Party
with a
Purpose

*Creative Ways to Share
the Love of Christ*

Page Hughes

new
hope
PUBLISHERS

Birmingham, Alabama

New Hope® Publishers
P. O. Box 12065
Birmingham, AL 35202-2065
www.newhopepubl.com

Library of Congress Cataloging-in-Publication Data
Hughes, Page.
Party with a purpose : creative ways to share the love of Christ / Page
Hughes.
p. cm.
ISBN 1-56309-806-7 (pbk.)
1.   Evangelistic work. 2. Parties-Religious aspects-Christianity.
I.   Title.
BV3793.H83 2003
241'.671—dc21
2003005084

Page layout design by Kathy Sealy

ISBN: 1-56309-806-7

N034122 • 0305 • 2M2

Dedication

To my husband Les
and children
Kyle
Caleb
Luke
and Dorothy Gené

and all the people
who helped me with this book.

You're my favorite people to party with!

Contents

Introduction

Welcome to *Party with a Purpose*. With preparation and prayer, you can pull off a fabulous party that may lead your guests to Christ. Inside you will find terrific party ideas that include:

- Helpful ideas for invitations to make
- Creative decorations that will be fun and support your theme
- Enjoyable activities to do at the party
- Tasty suggestions for refreshment and recipes
- Thoughtful devotions that support your theme and introduce your guests to a relationship with Christ
- Simple take-home favors to remember the occasion.

I hope you have a wonderful time giving these parties. Most of all, I hope many of your guests will begin an exciting new life in Christ. My goal is to see as many people as possible fall in love with Jesus.

Partying—Can Christians Do That?

The answer to the above question is *yes*! We can and we should. Jesus is our example, and He certainly enjoyed gathering together with others for the purpose of loving them into God's kingdom.

You may be thinking to yourself, "What do you mean when you say *partying*?" Many people attach to the word *partying* ideas of drinking, carousing, and the like. To me, partying is an opportunity to get together with others for a time of fun and fellowship. What makes *Party with a Purpose* unique is that our purpose is to get to know our guests and their needs, to become their friend, and eventually earn the right to share our faith in Jesus Christ. We

1

have found that people don't want to be your "project." They want to be your friend. Partying is one way we get to know others in our neighborhood or in our field of influence. Today we rarely take time or have opportunities to get to know those who live on either side of us, work at the same place, or even have children playing on the same athletic team. Partying encourages us to make opportunities to get to know others and celebrate our faith in Christ.

Another question you may be asking is, "Why should Christians celebrate their faith?" We are going to heaven one day and are experiencing abundant life here on earth. Now that's something to celebrate! So many today are looking for hope. We possess that hope. It is just a matter of communicating that hope to others. Partying gives us a platform to share the hope that we possess (1 Peter 3:15).

How? Now that is the question. Some of you may be thinking, "I am not good at planning parties." Not to worry. First I would encourage you to pray and ask God to lead you in what He would have you do. I have planned several parties for you. All you need to do is find the one that fits you and carry out the plan. You may discover that none are perfect for you. That's okay, too. This book gives you enough ideas that you can pick and choose and create your own.

Some of you may be thinking, "I could plan the party, or at least carry out someone else's plan, but I am not sure about how to share an evangelistic testimony." Again, I would encourage you to pray and seek the Lord. An evangelistic devotion is provided for each party that follows the party theme. If you are just getting to know your guests, after praying you may not feel led to share the devotion. That's fine, too. You may want to use your first time together to get acquainted. Remember you are working on building relationships and the privilege of sharing your faith. The most important thing is to pray and ask God to lead you (James 1:5). When the time is right, you may use the devotion provided or come up with your own, using this devotion as a guide. God will give you the words to say (Exodus 4:12). You may be a little timid, like Moses in Exodus. If so, don't let your timidity be a reason not to have a party. Look for a friend who is willing to share. If God is leading you, He will provide you with a partner.

Whether you are sharing the devotion or not, your guests should leave your home knowing you love Jesus. We give you ways to incorporate Scripture in everything from decorations to the favor they take home.

Let me take this opportunity to encourage you to use *Party with a Purpose* as a guide. Our greatest guide is the Holy Spirit, and if you ask, He will guide you (John 16:13), give you boldness (Acts 4:29), and help you with wonderfully creative ideas.

Jesus Loved a Good Party

Why did Jesus celebrate? I am firmly convinced that Jesus loved to celebrate because He knew it was the best way to reach people. The Bible reveals that Jesus performed the first miracle of His ministry at a wedding in Cana, in Galilee (John 2:1–11). He was often seen feasting with sinners, reclining with tax gatherers, and spending time with both religious people and sinners alike. Even His final meal with His disciples was a going-away party. Jesus truly loved people and wanted to meet not just their physical needs but also their spiritual needs. The best way to do that was to be where they were.

How did Jesus celebrate? We can see again from Jesus' last meal with His disciples that He knew some planning must take place (Mark 14:12–26). Jesus sent two disciples to prepare the Passover meal. He was a gracious host. He demonstrated this by serving His guests and meeting their needs. Whether He was washing their feet or breaking the bread, Jesus led with a servant spirit.

In addition to hosting a great party, Jesus was also a fabulous guest. He entertained by telling stories (Luke 8:4), He showed concern for His hosts (Luke 10:38–42), and He had time for everyone, including the children (Mark 10:13–16).

How did Jesus minister to others during times of celebration? Again, in the Gospels we observe Jesus giving physical and spiritual healing to those He met. Luke 4:38–39 records the story of Jesus healing Peter's mother-in-law. The Bible says she got up and waited on them. Can't you just see her getting up and making biscuits or something warm and wonderful to eat? Luke goes on to tell us, "the people brought to Jesus all who had various kinds of sicknesses, and laying his hands on each one, he healed them" (Luke 4:40). My favorite story has Jesus as an impromptu host. He had taught a crowd of over 5000 all day. Jesus was concerned about His guests' physical well-being. He wouldn't send them home without dinner. He made much out of little (does that sound like your house at times? It does mine!) and fed 5000 men, not counting women and children, with five loaves of bread and two fish.

Planning Your Party

Planning is important for a great party. I suggest you begin your party planning by praying and asking God to show you what He desires for you to do. We must have His power and leadership to make our party a success. He will also give you wisdom each step of the way to know what the theme should be, whom to invite, how to share, and many more details that must be considered.

Your next step is to let your spouse know what you believe God is leading you to do. Your family is a part of your party's success. Whether their part is cleaning, hosting, or relocating during the actual party, families need to feel a part.

As you begin to plan the actual party, there are many things to consider. First, what do you believe God is leading you to do? Look through the party ideas. Is there one that stands out in your mind? These are suggestions for where to start, but you can be creative and make the party your own. Consider whom God would have you invite. Do you have neighbors or co-workers you would like to know better? How about new people in your neighborhood? Or maybe there are people you have known for some time, but you are not sure where they will spend eternity. The possibilities are unlimited. Be open to God's leading and make a list of the people God brings to your mind. Now take the party theme that appealed to you and begin making your plans.

Discuss with your spouse the budget you will need to make the party a success. Keep in mind that you don't have to spend a lot of money to have a wonderful time. There are lots of fun ideas of things to do, recipes to prepare, and take-home favors to make that will not cost a lot of money. I tried to make these parties affordable, but if you have a smaller budget, you might use fewer decorations or have others help with refreshments. Another way to save is to use dishes, cups, and silver from your pantry rather than using disposable. If you have a larger budget, you may want to dream bigger. For your budget list, remember to include paper goods (including plates, napkins, utensils, cups), food, decorations, child care, cleaning costs, guest speaker's gift, articles needed for the "Just for Fun" section, and items needed for the take-home favors.

Now you are ready to set a date, choose a place, and make your invitation list. Again, make this a matter of prayer. Have a few friends over to pray with you. Then ask them to help you brainstorm about decorations and menu possibilities.

Pray and consider how you will make your party evangelistic. Will you have a devotion time? Will you deliver the devotion yourself or enlist someone else? If you are beginning a relationship with your guests, a devotion might be a bit strong. If our purpose is to develop relationships, could you use decorations or a take-home gift to proclaim the gospel message? Your purpose will be to get to know guests so that in the future you will earn the privilege to share.

As you get closer to your party, you will send your invitations, purchase groceries, beverages, and decor, determine whether you will need to rearrange furniture to allow for traffic flow, prepare food ahead of time if possible, and lightly clean your home. Your home doesn't have to be "white glove" clean. Your guests will relax if your home is messy enough to be comfortable, and clean enough to be enjoyed.

Prayer is the key to the success of your party. It will turn your fear into peace. Prayer will turn your timidity into boldness, and it will help you to remember that God is in charge and you are merely His messenger to your guests. God loved them so much that He sent Jesus just for them. He wants your party to be a success even more than you do. Success is when you have been obedient to what God tells you to do. Whether your guests respond to the gospel message is up to them. You are only responsible to share what God has given to you.

Fun Anytime Parties

Princess Party

Theme
We can be children of the King.

A Party For
Mothers and young daughters or adult women and their favorite "princesses"

Invitations
The invitations for this event could be a teacup. Or, because the verse is so long, you may just want to go with a traditional invitation that includes the following verse:

Front: *It's a Princess Party*
for you and me
No special attire
is even necessary.

Inside: *You are truly someone special,*
as special as can be.
If you have a little princess
and want to bring her, feel free.

Date: _____

Time: _____

Place: _____

RSVP: _____

Decorations

The decorations for this party will be full of fantasy and fun. You could use:

Tulle, tiaras, silver tea service, jewels, gloves, lots of silver, teacups, hats, dress up clothes, a red carpet, throne, scepter, old prom dresses, costume jewelry

You can have lots of fun with everything from entering on a red carpet to serving refreshments on fine china. Be a child again and pretend you are having a royal occasion with a few of your closest friends. The more fun you have, the more fun they will have.

Just for Fun

Dress up was always such fun as children. Whether your guests are children or adults, this can be a fun thing. Have hats, gloves, old jewelry (the gaudier, the better), boas, tiaras, robes, or anything fun to dress up in. If you are entertaining young guests, you can use old prom dresses, high-heeled shoes, silky nightgowns, or even an old slip. The idea is to just have fun. You can even have a camera (with film) available to remember the occasion.

Makeovers can be fun as well. You may want to invite a beauty consultant to come and do makeovers, or you may want to do your own. Most ladies enjoy having their nails done, even if you take turns doing each other's. The objective here is to fellowship and have fun.

Movie time! The movie *The Princess Diaries* is a wonderful, clean movie that young and old will really enjoy. It is about a young girl who finds out she is a real princess. Serve popcorn and drinks to your dressed-up guests and laugh a lot as you enjoy the movie.

Teach etiquette to your guests. You don't have to be Miss Manners to be able to pass along a few helpful pointers. Check out a book from the library and bone up on proper etiquette.

Devotion

Most little girls dream about being a princess. They imagine themselves wearing a crown, living in a huge mansion, and being married to a handsome prince. *The Princess Diaries* is a movie where a young girl comes to the realization that her father was the crown prince of a European country. She had been separated from him at birth and had no idea that she was the heir to the throne. Her grandmother comes to the young woman and informs her that she is the Princess of Genovia. After some rebellion and much training, she is ready to assume her position.

You might be thinking, "That could never happen." It could and it does. When we realize that the Creator and King of the universe created us, and that we are His children, we too come to the realization that we are royal heirs. The Bible says in 1 Peter 2:9, "But you are a chosen people, a royal priesthood, a holy nation, a people belonging to God, that you may declare the praises of him who called you out of darkness into his wonderful light."

You, my friend, are called out of darkness, which is the way of the world. God loved you so much that He gave Jesus so you could live in His light. You are chosen to be a part of God's royal family. Today you too can find out that your heavenly Father, who is the King, loves you and desires to make you a princess. You won't have a crown or a mansion here on earth, but it is coming. Jesus said in John 14:3, "And if I go and prepare a place for you, I will come back and take you to be with me that you also may be where I am." The Bible says that Jesus is the Prince of Peace (Isaiah 9:6). As you have read, He is coming back to get those who trust in Him. So friend, you too can have a royal experience of your own by accepting your heavenly Father's invitation to be a part of His royal family. I would be glad to talk to you later if you would like to know more.

Refreshments
- Royal Scones (*recipe in back*)
- Friendship Tea (*recipe in back*)
- Petite Sandwiches (*recipe in back*)
- Popcorn and soft drinks (theater-style foods)

Taking It Home

Tiara: These can be purchased in the party section of a department store or at any party store. You might attach a card that says, "You are special to God and me."

Sachet: You can make a sachet using a 9 x 9-inch square of tulle, a sweet-smelling potpourri, and 5 inches of ribbon. You might attach a small card that says, "You are chosen." —1 Peter 2:9

Princess Diary: Go to a dollar store and purchase an inexpensive journal for each of your guests. Inside the cover, thank them for coming to your Princess Party and write 1 Peter 2:9.

Life's a Circus,
Come Join the Fun

Theme
Spiritual growth

A Party For
Elementary-age children

Invitations
Circus tents would be a great invitation idea. Fold a piece of construction paper in half. Cut the paper into the shape of tent, placing the left side of the tent on the fold. This will form a card when opened.

> **Front:** *Hurry, Hurry, One and All*
> **Inside:** *Come join the circus and have a ball*

Date: _____

Time: _____

Place: _____

RSVP: _____

Decorations

Tent, streamers, clowns, stuffed animals, popcorn bags or containers, three rings

Just for Fun

Pin the nose on the clown—Draw or purchase a picture of a clown's face. Cut out red circles from construction paper for noses. You will need a blindfold to cover the contestants' eyes as they spin around and try to pin or tape the nose of the clown in the correct spot. A great prize would be a rubber clown's nose for the winner.

Wild animal relay—Divide your guests into equal teams. Assign each team member an animal. The object of the game is to move like your animal as you race to a mark on the other end of the playing area and race back. The next contestant is tagged and the game continues until all contestants have completed the race. The winning team is the one that finishes first. Ties are broken by a judge who determines which team did the best animal impersonations. The prize for this game could be a box of animal cookies to be shared by the winning team.

Peanut toss—For this game you will need roasted peanuts in the shell and a small bucket. Depending on the age and ability of the contestants, mark off a distance away from the bucket from which to toss the peanuts. You may choose more than one tossing line depending on the age range of your participants. (It is easiest if you make a tape mark for the tossing line.) Players go one at a time, and each is given 10 peanuts to toss into the bucket. The winner is the one who gets the most peanuts in the bucket.

Devotion

The Greatest Lion Tamer

What comes to your mind when you think of a circus? (Allow time for responses.) We can think of so many things that remind us of the circus, but the one I want to concentrate on today is the lion tamer. It is amazing how he can stand in the cage with the king of the jungle and show no fear. I have pondered why he shows such confidence. One reason is because he has prepared. He has studied the great beast and knows his habits and temperament. He has also practiced time and time again with the lions and anticipates their every move. He shows them who is in control, and through his voice and actions he commands them to do his bidding.

There is a biblical character who comes to mind when I think of lions. His name is Daniel. His story is found in the Book of Daniel, chapter six. Daniel lived in a time when it was not popular to follow God. He was a devoted follower of God. The first few chapters of Daniel tell us that Daniel had a close relationship with God. He studied and knew about God. It was his daily practice to talk to God, and God was pleased with Daniel. But praying got Daniel in trouble. Some leaders in the country were jealous of Daniel and asked the king to make a new law: everyone must pray to the king only or be thrown into the lions' den. Daniel prayed to God only, and he was ordered to be thrown into the lions' den. But Daniel was not afraid. He knew that God would take care of him whether he lived or died. God, the greatest lion tamer of all, closed the mouths of the ferocious animals, and the next morning when Daniel left the den without a scratch, the king knew Daniel's God was the one true God.

Do your friends and mine know the one true God? Do we lead them to Him by the way we act? Daniel found daily time with God to be a necessity. That is why he had peace when the lions in his life came. We may not have *real* ferocious beasts breathing down our necks, but each of us face demands each day. I want to challenge you to be like Daniel. Get to know God in a more intimate way by studying His Word and talking to Him daily. If you have any questions about how or where to start, I would be glad to speak to you later about it.

If there is one thing I have learned over the last few years, it is that life is nuts (show the take-home bag of peanuts), and we should not try to handle it without God. I hope that when the lions of your life come you will find great peace.

Refreshments

- Animal crackers
- Cracker Jacks
- Peanuts
- Popcorn
- Cotton candy

Taking It Home

Small paper bag of roasted peanuts in the shell. Attach a small sticker or tag that says, "Life is nuts—don't try it without God."

Hook, Line, and Sinker

Theme
Fishing, fun, and the gospel

A Party For
Families, or fathers and sons, or any group of people who like to fish!

Invitations
Cut out fish-shaped invitations from construction paper.

Front: *Bring your hook, line, and sinker*
Inside: *Join us for an afternoon of fun.*

Date: _____
Time: _____
Place: _____
RSVP: _____

Another idea would be to send a card with a hook, line, and sinker attached and the above information.

Decorations

Decorations for this party will vary depending on where you choose to have it. If you have a pond available, it would be great fun to have an afternoon of fishing. This outing would require few decorations besides what nature provides! You might want to serve your refreshments using Styrofoam coolers, tackle boxes, or picnic basket items.

If a pond or lake is not available, your decorations must set the atmosphere. Some items you may want to consider are: boat, fishing lures, spools of fishing line, net, tackle box, fishing poles, fishing hat, stringer, minnow bucket, cricket keeper, real goldfish in a fishbowl for a centerpiece, child's swimming pool, gummy worms, driftwood, bobbers, plastic worms, life preservers.

Just for Fun

Again, this will depend on where you have your party. If it is at a lake, the fun will be actually fishing. Have on hand an extra pole or two and some extra bait. Be sure to consider safety for your guests, and if you allow guests to use a boat, life vests must be worn by everyone in the boat.

If your party is at a home, there are still some fun things you can do.

Video fish by renting a fishing game from your area video store. If your family does not have a game system, these too may be rented from the video store. The men and boys in your group will really enjoy this.

Kids' pond is made by using a child's swimming pool or by taping off a pretend pond. Cut construction paper fish of varying sizes. You may want to put Bible verses on the fish to be read as they are caught. Put a paper clip in each fish's mouth. Make a fishing pole by attaching a string to a dowel rod (you may need more than one, depending on the number of young children you have). Hot glue or tie a magnet to the end of your string to be your hook. Then have lots of fun as you "fish" for paper fish. Please be sure to throw back your fish. They are not big enough to eat (ha ha).

Fish tales is a fun game your guests will enjoy. Ask your guests to share their favorite fish tale. The tale doesn't have to be about them. Have an award for the best story.

Devotion

Isn't fishing fun? Whether you are out in a boat on a calm placid lake, on a pond bank with your favorite fishing buddy, or even playing a video version of the sport, fishing is fun. It is a challenge to lure a creature into thinking the bait is something he wants or even needs. Then as soon as that little creature bites down on that bait, he finds he is caught in something he can't get out of. Then you reel that creature in and, well, we know what can happen then. Let's just say it's often the end of the road for him.

Be careful or you too may find yourself tricked into the frying pan. God has a plan for you. He desires that we live in freedom, peace, and joy. Yet from days of old everyone from Eve on down has been lured by Satan's bait. Ephesians 4:27 says, "Do not give the devil a foothold." We must turn from that bait though it looks like it promises great things. Turn to the only One who can give true freedom—and that's Jesus. There will come an end of time. Where will you find yourself? Will it be on Satan's stringer or swimming in God's pool of life? If you would like to know more about how you can know for sure, please talk to me later.

Refreshments

❧ Hook, Line, and Sinker Dip *(recipe in back)*
❧ Tuna sandwiches

- Goldfish crackers
- Gummy worms
- Lemonade served in a small fishing cooler
- Fisherman's Folly *(recipe in back)*

Taking It Home

Catch of the day: Make these fun party favors by cutting tulle into 9-inch squares. Put a handful of goldfish crackers in the center of your square, then bring the sides to the center and tie off with a piece of fishing line.

Fabulous Friends

Theme
A friend loves at all times.

A Party For
Women

Invitations
Your invitations can be as simple as homemade paper dolls or even a heart cut from construction paper. You could even use a valentine as your invitation. Be creative. We suggest:

Front: *Fabulous Friend*
Inside: *Come help me celebrate*
Friendship

Date: _____
Time: _____
Place: _____
RSVP: _____

P.S. Bring your purse and a smile (for a scavenger hunt)

Decorations

Decorations for this party can be anything feminine. Choose a direction and go with it. Some suggestions are: hearts, cupids, valentine decorations, dolls, dress-up clothes, hats, old jewelry, tulle, teacups, pearls, fresh flowers (tulips, paperwhites, daffodils). Decorating for this one should be fun. Let your imagination take over like you did when you were a child. If it's feminine and pretty, it will be wonderful.

Just for Fun

Purse scavenger hunt—Have the ladies get out their purses. The object of the game is to see how many of the items called out are in your purse. For each item you find you get a point. The item to be found will be preceded by a statement a true friend might say to you.

- I will help you when you are in need. —*Safety pin*
- I am always ready for fun. —*Checkbook*
- I would give you my last cent. —*A penny*
- You can trust me. —*A credit card*
- I would never brush you off. —*A brush*
- We stick together through thick and thin. —*Old piece of candy*
- Though you may mess up, I will always forgive you. —*Pencil eraser*
- You are on my list of people I can't do without. —*Shopping list*
- I am here when you hurt. —*Band-Aid*
- My days just wouldn't be the same without you. —*Calendar*
- I have trouble keeping up with my life; that's why God sent you. —*Palm Pilot*
- When you are hurting, I will cry with you. —*Kleenex (extra point if used)*
- I think you are picture perfect. —*Pictures*

- Write it down: I am proud of you. —***Pen***
- No need to change; I like you like you are. —***Change purse***
- Nail it down: I am glad you are my friend. —***Nail file***
- You color my world more beautiful. —***Any kind of makeup***

You may wish to award the lowest scores ("Traveling Light Award") and the highest scores ("Prepared for Everything Award"). Everyone is a winner when they have a friend.

Favorite friend story—For this activity, you will need a bag of Skittles. Each friend takes one Skittle. She will tell a story depending on what color of Skittle she gets. You can tell a story about a friend who is not at the party.

Red: The craziest thing a friend and you ever did.

Green: A difficult time when your friend was there for you.

Yellow: Your favorite thing your friend and you do.

Orange: An adventure you would like for your friend and you to do.

Purple: The very best thing about your friend.

Devotion

What are some of the things that endear your friends to you? Some of the things that endear my friends to me are: they are there when I need them; they are interested in the things happening in my life; and when I have a need, if there is any way they can possibly meet it, they will. I am very blessed to have my friends.

I also have another Friend. He knows me even better than my best friend. He knows exactly what I am thinking. He comforts me when I hurt. He knows what I need even before I do and is already at work supplying that need even as I ask. He forgives me when I hurt Him and when I say things I don't truly mean. He knows the desires of my heart and is just waiting to give them to me. He directs me in paths I need to go down, not just the ones I want to take. The Bible says in John 15:13, "Greater love has no one than this, that he lay down his life for his friends." That is what my friend did for me. He is truly out for my very best.

You may be wondering why I haven't introduced you to Him yet, and if He is so wonderful, why haven't you seen Him? My friend is Jesus. I asked Him to be my friend and to forgive me of all the bad that I have done. I told Him that if He would have me, I would allow Him to lead me and be my friend the rest of my life. He now is my master as well as my friend, and today as we celebrate friendship, I wanted to introduce Him to you. I hope you have seen Him in me when I have spoken a kind word or done a good deed for you. He desires to be your best friend, too. All you have to do is admit you have done wrong things in your life and ask Him to forgive you. Then allow Him to direct your paths, too. I would be glad to talk to you later about how you can do this.

Refreshments
- Friendship Bread *(recipe in back)*
- Tea Time Cookies *(recipe in back)*
- Friendship Tea *(recipe in back)*

Taking It Home
A cord with a note attached that reads . . .
A cord of three strands is not easily broken.
When you are at the end of your rope,
God and I will be here for you. —Ecclesiastes 4:9–12

Bookmark: Make a bookmark that has John 15:13: "Greater love has no one than this, that he lay down his life for his friends."

Friendship bread starter and recipe: If you enjoy baking, consider making a small loaf of friendship bread for each guest to take home. You may want to make bread starter available to your guests along with instructions on how to make the bread. A cute addition to this would be a note that reads, "Man does not live on bread alone, but on every word that comes from the mouth of God."—Matthew 4:4.

Beat the Blues

Theme
Encouragement

A Party For
Youth or adults

Invitations
Been feeling a little blue lately?
Come help us Beat the Blues.
Put on something blue and join us
As we break out of the doldrums.

Date: _____
Time: _____
Place: _____
RSVP: _____

Decorations

Anything blue—blue plates, cups, napkins, and silver-ware, blue carnations, blue suede shoes, Blue's Clues dog, anything you can think of . . . and play blues music.

Just for Fun

Blue elephant swap—Did you ever receive a gift and wonder, "What will I ever do with this?" These are wonderful items for a blue elephant swap. Each guest brings one item they no longer want. The items are wrapped and are exchanged as gifts. All of the blue elephant gifts are put into a pile. Before the game begins, numbers are written and cut apart for the number of participants in the game. Each participant draws a number. The game begins when the player with #1 opens a gift from the blue elephant gift pile. It is then player #2's turn. Player #2 can open a gift from the pile or take player #1's gift. If #2 takes #1's gift, #1 opens another gift from the pile. If #2 chooses to open a gift from the pile, it then becomes player #3's turn. Player #3 can choose to open a gift from the pile or steal from one of the other players. A gift can only be stolen two times; the item then is frozen. Play continues until all players have an opportunity to choose a gift or steal. At the end of the game, everyone takes home a "treasure."

Beyond the blues—Get as many toothpicks as you have guests. Color one end of each toothpick one of four colors with colored markers. The host or hostess will hold the toothpicks in such a way that the colored ends are hidden. Each guest picks a toothpick. The guest is to answer the question that corresponds with the color selected. You may choose questions other than the ones below if it will better suit your guests. The purpose is to get to know each other better and to look toward the positive.

Light blue: What experience are you glad is behind you?

Navy blue: What is one experience you would like to have again?

Aqua blue: What one place would you like to go to this year?

Royal blue: What is one thing you would like to do if money were no object?

Devotion

Psalm 143:7–8 reads, "Come quickly, LORD, and answer me, for my depression deepens. Don't turn away from me, or I will die. Let me hear of your unfailing love to me in the morning, for I am trusting you. Show me where to walk, for I have come to you in prayer" (NLT).

The man who first penned these words was David. The Bible says he was a man after God's own heart. You would think that this man who loved God and was the king of Israel would not get "blue" or depressed. Yet here in Psalm 143 he says he is depressed. When you read the Book of Psalms you find that David battled the blues many times. Yet David also gives us a clue as to how he beat the blues. David asked God to let him hear of God's unfailing love to him in the morning. This verse would indicate that David spent time with God in the morning. You, like David, can be assured that your heavenly Father loves you with unfailing love. The psalm also indicates that though David might have felt uncertain of future events, he trusted God and asked God to show him where to walk. The close of the passage indicates that David knew the way to access his power source was to come to God in prayer.

If the circumstances of your life have you feeling a little "blue," take David's advice: spend time with God, know that He loves you, pray to Him, and trust Him to show you the next step. David put it this way in Psalm 51: "Restore to me again the joy of your salvation, and make me willing to obey you" (NLT).

We have a little treat for you to take home. (Have snack size Almond Joy candy bars with this verse attached: "The joy of the LORD is your strength" —Nehemiah 8:10.) If you are blue today, you can beat the blues by claiming this verse and practicing what David did, for "the joy of the Lord is my strength."

Refreshments

Anything blue or that can be turned blue with food coloring. Some possibilities are blueberry muffins, blue tortilla chips, cheesecake with blueberry topping, or salads with blue cheese dressing.

Taking It Home

Almond Joy candy bars with this verse attached:
   "The joy of the LORD is your strength" —Nehemiah 8:10

Buttons and Beaus

Theme
Introduction party

A Party For
Couples—often women know each other through church, work, or parenting responsibilities, but they don't know each other's families. This party is an opportunity for couples to get to know each other.

Invitations
Button up your overcoat and
Bring your Beau to our
Buttons and Beaus Party (or Barbecue)

Date: _____
Time: _____
Place: _____
RSVP: _____

Decorations

To dress up the party, decorate with buttons, bows, cufflinks, pearls, dress-up jewelry, candles, and a formal table setting.

To dress it down for a barbecue, use gingham, bows, old buttons, and plasticware wrapped in napkins and tied with bows. Make placecards with buttons on the guy's cards and bows and the girl's cards.

Just for Fun

M&M game—Get a bag of M&M candy. Have people choose two different-colored M&Ms. Ask them not to eat the M&Ms, but to wait for instructions. If they are holding a:

Green: Tell where you went on your first date with your spouse (or at least a date that you can remember).

Red: Tell where you grew up and a favorite childhood memory.

Orange: Tell about the most embarrassing thing that has ever happened to you.

Brown: Tell what your favorite movie is and why.

Yellow: If you could change professions and be anything you wanted to be, what profession would you choose?

Button flip—place a cup at one end of playing area. Mark off a challenging flipping distance. Flip buttons with the objective of making them land inside the cup.

Bow relay—Divide your guests into teams of six. If you don't have six for each team, have a team member do more than one task. Teams line up. One at a time, they run to a table or flat surface at the opposite end of playing area and perform their assigned task. Once their task is complete, they run back to the line and tag the next person in line, who then runs down and completes their task. Play continues until the package is delivered to the line leader.

Tasks:
Player 1 places button in box.
Player 2 tapes the box closed.
Player 3 cuts wrapping paper.
Player 4 wraps the box.
Player 5 ties a bow on the box.
Player 6 delivers the wrapped box to the line leader.

Devotion

There is no formal devotion for this party. The purpose is to build relationships with your newfound friends. The best way to know where people are spiritually is to get to know them. During the evening you may want to get to know your guests by asking them questions. The following are great conversation starters:

- Are you originally from this area?
- Where do you work? What do you do there?
- Where did you go to school?
- Where do you attend church?

As you find out more about your friends, introduce them to others in the family of faith who may have similar backgrounds or professions. Affirm them if they already attend church, and invite them to yours if they do not.

Refreshments

Formal—Shrimp and white sauce over bow-tie pasta
Dressed-down—Barbecue with button cookies for dessert (sugar cookies with icing used to make them look like buttons)

Taking It Home

Button and bow ornament: This is a very simple ornament made from a ribbon bow with a button sewn in the center. Attach a piece of gold thread, and you have a button and bow ornament.

Ministry Parties

Stitch in Time
(Quilting Party)

Theme
Mentoring by teaching a life skill

A Party For
Women who like to quilt or want to learn how

Invitations
The time has come for lots of fun
Bring some thread, and I'll bring some
A stitch or two may not seem like much to you
But together we will create something new.

Date: _____

Time: _____

Place: _____

RSVP: _____

Decorations

Quilts, quilting frame or needlepoint hoops, thread, fabric, needles, backing, thimbles.

Just for Fun

The ladies will make a square to be made into a quilt. The hostess should provide squares to be quilted and invite someone who quilts to teach the ladies how. The squares can be put together to make a quilt to be used in the church nursery or for a mission project.

Quilt review—As a part of the party you may want to do a quilt review. Guests can bring quilts made by themselves or others to show. You will need an area to display the quilts, and something (chairs, small tables) to display them on.

Devotion

Share the parable of the Patchwork Heart, taken from the book *The Patchwork Heart* by Kim Moore and Pam Mellskog (NavPress, 2002, www.navpress.com).

One day a young woman stood in the town square and proclaimed that she had the most beautiful heart in the whole valley. A large crowd gathered, and they all admired her heart, for it was perfect, the most beautiful heart they had ever seen. There was not a mark or a flaw in it. The young woman was very proud and boasted all the more loudly. Suddenly, an old woman appeared at the front of the crowd.

"Why, your heart is not nearly as beautiful as mine," she said. The crowd and the young woman looked at the old woman's heart. It was beating strongly, but full of scars. It had places where pieces had been removed and other pieces put in. But they didn't fit quite right, and jagged edges abounded. In fact, in some places there were deep gouges where whole pieces were missing. The people stared and wondered how she could say her heart was more beautiful. When the young woman looked more closely at the old woman's heart, she laughed.

"You must be joking," she said. "Compare your heart with mine. Mine is perfect, and yours is a mess."

"Yes," agreed the old woman. "Yours is perfect-*looking*, but I would never trade. You see, every scar represents a person to whom I have given my love. I tear out a piece of my heart and give it to her, and often she gives me a piece of her heart that fits into the empty space. But because the pieces aren't exact I have some rough edges, which I cherish because they remind me of the love we shared.

"Sometimes I have given away pieces of my heart and the other person hasn't returned a piece of her heart to me. These are the empty gouges. Giving love is taking a chance. Although these gouges are painful, they stay open and remind me of the love I have for these people too. Perhaps someday they may yet fill the space I have waiting. So now do you see what true beauty is?"

The young woman stood silently with tears running down her cheeks. She approached the old woman, reached into her own perfect and beautiful heart, and with trembling hands offered the old woman a generous piece.

The old woman accepted this offering and placed it in her heart, then took a piece from her scarred heart and placed it in the fresh wound of the young woman's heart. It fit, but not perfectly. There were some jagged edges.

The young woman looked at her heart, imperfect as it now was, and realized that it was more beautiful than ever. The two women embraced and walked away, side by side.
—Adapted, author unknown

My prayer is that you all will have a beautiful patchwork heart.

Refreshments
- Tea Time Cookies *(recipe in back)*
- Punch
- Finger sandwiches

Taking It Home

Patchwork heart ornament
Bible marker with a patchwork heart

Hurricane Party

Theme

Mission Project

If you live near the coast, hurricanes are a real threat. When the warning goes out, why not prepare to meet the needs that may arise? Shelters will need blankets and canned foods or snack foods, and evacuees will need batteries and water once they return. Contact a local relief agency to see what they need, or call the local American Red Cross. All gifts during a crisis will be appreciated.

A Party For
Adults, youth, or families

Invitations
The wind is blowing and the sky is getting black
A storm is brewing and we need your help to pack
Grab some batteries or a blanket for our sack
Help us prepare for a hurricane
So our friends will not lack.

(Provide a list of suggested items to bring to the party as a donation. Inform the group where the items will be sent.)

Date: _____

Time: _____

Place: _____

RSVP: _____

Decorations

Hurricane lamps, flashlights, blankets, weather radio, matches, water, canned goods

Just for Fun

The main activity for this party will be collecting and organizing emergency items to be donated to a relief agency in the area. For additional fun, plan some games such as the following.

Name a hurricane—Divide your guests into teams. Read the following news release. "The national weather service comes up with a list of names for hurricanes each year. This year the list was misplaced. It's up to you and your teammates to come up with a list of possible hurricane names. Go through the alphabet and make a list of names for this year's storms. Start with A and go to Z, giving one name per letter. Awards will be given to the team who finishes first and the one who has the most creative names."

Flashlight tag—If your party includes young people, this may be a fun game. You will need a large yard and a flashlight. One person is "It." Everyone hides while the person who is "It" counts to 100. When "It" gets to 100, they turn on the flashlight and then go to try to find the other players. The way others are tagged is by the light from the flashlight that "It" carries. If the light shines on a contestant, they are out of the game until the next game begins. The game continues until all contestants are found. The last person found becomes "It" for the next game.

The wind and the fury—This game is a relay game. Divide your guests into two equal teams. The object of the game is to blow a ping-pong ball or a feather to a chosen spot on the opposite end of the playing area. The contestant picks up the ball or feather and runs it back to the next contestant in line. Play continues until all contestants have completed the relay.

Devotion

Have you ever experienced a hurricane? The National Weather Service is excellent at predicting and preparing for these giant storms. We have even identified a "hurricane season" when conditions are right for hurricanes. When a tropical depression or storm forms, the NWS tracks it and tells us where it is likely to make landfall. The residents of the target area are advised to cover or tape windows to protect them from flying glass and debris. They may be asked to move to higher ground. People make a mad dash to local stores to buy tape, batteries, plywood, flashlights, radios, candles, and water. Even people miles away from the coast empty grocery store shelves, knowing that tornadoes spawned by the mother storm can cause havoc. Bathtubs are filled with water to be used in case the water system is polluted, and outdoor furniture or equipment is secured. After all preparations are made, people sit back and ride out the storm. Tension is usually so thick you can feel it all around you.

The Bible tells us in Luke 8:22–25 of a time when Jesus and his disciples were caught in the middle of a raging storm. The disciples and their Master were en route to the other side of the Sea of Galilee. Jesus fell asleep as their vessel cast off. During the course of the trip, a torrential storm tossed and turned the tiny ship. The disciples began to panic and say, "Master, Master, we're going to drown!" (v. 24). Jesus got up and charged the wind and the waves to be still. The storm subsided. Then Jesus asked, "Where is your faith?" In fear and amazement the disciples asked one another, "Who is this? He commands even the winds and the water, and they obey him" (v. 25). Today your hurricane may not be an actual rainstorm. You may be experiencing a storm in your finances, your emotions, or even in your spiritual life. Regardless of what kind of storm you are facing, know that the same one who commands the winds and the waves controls the storms of your life as well. He wants you to have peace. Jesus is saying to you and me what He said to his disciples: "Where is your faith?" He can and will bring peace in your storm as well. (Close with prayer.)

Refreshments
- Peanut butter crackers
- Lemonade
- Cheese and crackers
- Vegetable soup

Taking It Home
A plastic tumbler or glass that says, "I survived the storm." (If you are doing this during an actual storm, include the name of the hurricane, i.e. "I survived Camille.")

Theme
Encouraging a cancer patient

A Party For
Women—This party is meant to encourage a cancer patient who is undergoing chemotherapy.

Invitations
Hats off to our special friend
Join us for a "Hat Shower"
In _____'s honor

Date: _____
Time: _____
Place: _____
RSVP: _____

(Please come wearing your own unique hat creation. Prizes will be given.)

Decorations

Hats, teacups, teapots, tulle, pearls, anything girlie and uplifting.

Just for Fun

Hat parade—Have friends come in a creative hat that they have made. Give prizes for most creative, most unusual, prettiest, most useful, and any other fun categories you can invent.

Make miniature hats—Items needed: 6.4 ounce Styrofoam cups, acrylic paints and paint brushes, small artificial flowers, small pearls, and thin ribbon to decorate hats. Preheat oven to 350 degrees. Put cups on a cookie sheet and place in oven until melted down into shape of a hat (this takes about 30 seconds). Paint with acrylic paints. This should be done before the party so that the hats will be ready for decorating. It will take a few hours for the hats to dry. At the party you will want to complete the hats using small artificial flowers, pearls, ribbons, feathers, or anything that is small and would complete the hat.

Devotion

We are here to honor our friend _____.
We all love her and have shared happy times with her.
(Enlist someone ahead of time to tell about a funny thing that happened with her and the honoree.) I have asked
_____ to share with us about a funny experience she and _____ had.
(Enlist another guest to share a time when the honoree was there for them in a time of trouble.) I have asked
_____ to share with us a time when _____ was there for her.

As you all know, _____ is a special friend to us all. We want to take a few minutes today to pray for _____ and to ask

God to strengthen her and give her peace as she walks through these challenging days. *(Prearrange for someone to lead in prayer or lead prayer yourself.)*

Today we have made these hats. The purpose of the hat is to remind us to pray for our friend. I would like for you to take the hat and this card home with you. The card reads:

When you see this hat of prayer
May you know He's always there,
Listening for your every care,
Handling what you cannot bear.

When you see your little hat, remember to pray for our precious friend.

Refreshments

☙ Baked Brims *(recipe in back)*
☙ Party Punch *(recipe in back)*
☙ Petite Sandwiches *(recipe in back)*

Taking It Home

The take-home gifts are prayer reminders—the miniature hats the ladies made and decorated. Let them attach a card with the following poem:

When you see this hat of prayer
May you know He's always there,
Listening for your every care,
Handling what you cannot bear.

Seasonal Parties

Spring Fling
Perennial Party

Theme
God makes everything beautiful in its time (Ecclesiastes 3:11).

A Party For
Women (or women and men) interested in gardening

Invitations
The invitations for this party can be lots of fun to create. You could use a packet of flower seeds as an invitation. Glue your invitation to the back. You could also hand-deliver small plants to each door. Buy a 6-pack of spring flowers to be planted. Cut them apart and wrap them individually in tissue paper. Use a small craft stick and glue your invitation to it. We suggest the following invitation.

Front: *Spring has sprung . . .*
Inside: *Now it's time for fun!*

Date: _____
Time: _____
Place: _____
RSVP: _____

Please bring bulbs or cuttings from your yard to share. If you don't have a perennial, don't worry. Come and let us share with you.

Decorations

Your yard is a wonderful place to start when you think of decor for this party. You may use anything from wheelbarrows to old pots. Keep the garden in mind and use things that you already have. Maybe the following will give you some ideas: spring flowers, gloves, pots, bird houses, spades, shovels, trowels, fountains, bulb planters, bird baths, bulbs, seeds, baskets.

Just for Fun

Ask a guest gardener or someone in your community with a green thumb to come and give helpful information about spring flower gardening. You could even let your friends know he or she is coming and encourage them to bring questions they would like answered. You could ask an area florist to come and give hints on arranging flowers. She might even do an arrangement as she speaks.

If I were a flower—In this game you ask your guests, "If you were a flower, what kind would you be and why?"

Bloomers—The object of this game is to match as many flowers as you can with the hostess. It's a "read my mind" or "read my list" kind of game. Give your guests a piece of paper and ask them to list eight different types of flowers. When you have given them time to work on their list, begin reading the list below, and ask women to check off each matching flower on their list. The one who matches all eight flowers on her list first, wins. Have a small bouquet of flowers put in a bag that your guests cannot see into. At the end of the game, ask the lady who matched all of her flowers first to "model" the bloomers. She may be a tad embarrassed until she opens the bag and finds she gets to model a beautiful bouquet.

Aster	Crocus
Gardenia	Jasmine
Portulaca	Zinnia
Holly	Morning Glory
Impatiens	Clematis
Azalea	Chrysanthemum
Geranium	Marigold
Snapdragon	Tulips
Peony	Petunia
Buttercup	Nasturtium
Sunflower	Christmas Cactus
Rose	Forget-Me-Not
Gladiola	Four-O-Clocks
Fuschia	Orchids
Hyacinth	Peace Lily
Violet	Daisy
Hibiscus	Dandelion
Iris	Phlox
Juniper	Daffodil
Carnation	Pansy
Baby's Breath	Gerbera Daisy
Lilac	Wisteria

Devotion

Tulips, spider lilies, azaleas, and daffodils all remind us that spring has sprung. Oh, the joy that new life brings after a season of barrenness and apparent deadness. We know life is returning. We are sharing flowers today that represent what seems to be dead and gone. The perennial "dies back" for the winter. What we see with the eye is dead, lifeless foliage. We cannot see what is happening within the bulb of the plant where it is resting and preparing to bring forth new life.

This reminds me of Jesus. The body of Jesus was lifeless as the soldiers took Him down from the cross. What they did not know was that He, too, would live again. On the third day after He died, God raised Jesus from His dead state. He conquered death so that we might live. John says Jesus died once for all and that if we love Him and do what He wants, we may live forever. We, too, one day will die. The question is, what will happen then? Will you live again with Jesus in Heaven? If you would like to know more about how you can be sure about where you will spend eternity, please talk to me later. I would be glad to answer any questions you have.

Refreshments
- Dirt Dessert (*recipe in back*)
- Gummy worms candy
- Cookies decorated with edible pansies—put a dollop of canned icing on a sugar cookie, then top with a pansy.
- Mint tea—Serve warm or iced tea with fresh mint in it. Fresh herbs are wonderful perennials.

Taking It Home
Exchange bulbs brought by guests. Be sure to have some extras in case your guests did not bring theirs. Make **plant cards** with Ecclesiastes 3:11, "He has made everything beautiful in its time," written on them. These can be made by using small cards and plastic cardholders like those used by florists to attach cards to arrangements.

ABCs and 123s

Theme
Back to the basics

A Party For
Adults or families

Invitations

Make a "blackboard" using a brown and black construction paper. First, cut a 4x6 inch piece of brown construction paper. Then cut a 3x5 inch piece of black construction paper. Glue the black onto the brown and you have a blackboard. Use a white gel pen to write on the black construction paper, and you have an easy invitation. This will be a one-sided invitation.

ABCs and 123s
It's a Back-to-School BASH!

Date: _____
Time: _____
Place: _____
RSVP: _____

Come wearing your school colors!

Decorations

The decorations for this event could include anything having to do with school: notebooks, old annuals, rulers, school boxes, lunch boxes, chalkboards, pencils, pens, crayons, chalk, notecards, erasers, apples, buses, old photos, school colors, school mascot, books.

Just for Fun

Your activities will be determined by your intended guest list. If this is an adults-only party, you would go with "Remember when" activities. If you have invited families, you would want to gear it more toward your younger audience. Here are suggestions for both.

Remember when—Have your guests bring old annuals or old photos of their school days. See if you can pick out your friends in their old photos.

Spin the bottle (rated G version)—Use an old bottle of any kind. Have your guests sit in a circle. Spin the bottle on a hard surface, and when it lands pointing to one of your guests, have that person answer one of the following questions: What was your best school memory? What was your most embarrassing school memory? What was your greatest fear when you were in school? Who was your first sweetheart? or What was the most interesting thing you learned in school?

Photo frame—(Provide adult supervision for children doing this craft.) Purchase wide craft sticks and glue them together, using hot glue, to make a frame. Have art items there for the children to decorate their frame. You may want to purchase some small letters and numbers to help them remember this special day. Encourage them to have their parents take a picture on the first day of school and put it in their frame.

Write a teacher—Encourage the children to write a letter thanking their teachers for teaching them this year. You may want to have extra paper and markers available and encourage them to make bookmarks for their teachers to include with their notes.

Bob for apples—Have a bucket of water and apples and let the children bob for the apples. No hands, please!

Devotion

How many of you have a child, grandchild, niece, nephew, or neighbor starting school soon? The beginning of the school year brings back so many memories. Do you remember the anticipation of finding out who your teacher would be, or the excitement of finding out your best friend was in your class? Do you remember shopping for the perfect outfit for the first day of class, or the first day "butterflies" that felt more like small bats as you tried to sleep the night before? The beginning of school brings back so many memories for me. My favorite was getting new supplies. Everything was new, unused, with not a scratch or stray mark on it. The pencils were full length and had never been sharpened. The workbooks were totally empty, waiting for me to fill them with letters and numbers as the days passed. Getting brand new notebooks had to top it all. They were spotless and unmarked—a far cry from the tattered and torn pages left from the year before.

Those notebooks are a wonderful illustration of what God can and will do in our lives. He takes the tattered and torn remnants of your life and gives you a brand new heart when you follow His ABC's.

A—Admit that you have done wrong.

B—Believe that Jesus can forgive you of that wrong.

C—Confess that wrong to Him and ask Him to forgive you and give you a new start.

Then look to Jesus, our great teacher, and follow His example. If you are interested in knowing more about how you can have this new start, I would be glad to answer any questions you have later. (Close with prayer for those who will soon be starting school.)

Refreshments

- Campbell's vegetarian vegetable soup with ABCs and 123s in it. This could be a wonderful appetizer or the main course.
- You may want to serve your refreshments in brown lunch sacks, filled with fun lunch food.
- Peanut butter and jelly sandwiches (you can have lunch meat available also)
- Small bags of chips
- Apples or a snack cake
- If you have invited families, why not try a potluck dinner?

Taking It Home

Photo frame: Families take home the photo frames the children have made.

New notebook: Give a new pocket-size notebook to each of your guests. On the first page of the notebook write 2 Corinthians 5:17— "If anyone is in Christ, he is a new creation; the old has gone, the new has come!"

Gridiron Grill

Theme
Football and the game of life

A Party For
Youth or adults

Invitations
A football-shaped invitation would be perfect.

Front: *It's a Gridiron Grill*
Inside: *Bring something to throw on the grill*
And join in the fun.

Date: _____
Time: _____
Place: _____
RSVP: _____

Come wearing your team colors!

Decorations

The decorations for this event would include anything representing your favorite sports team or anything having to do with football. Some suggestions are: footballs, pom-poms, helmets, recordings of team fight songs, megaphones, letter jackets, pennants, jerseys, cleats, team mascots or symbols, tailgate party items.

Just for Fun

Autograph party—As your guests arrive, give them a game card with the following statements on it. Have your guests find someone at the party who can answer truthfully to each statement, and have them sign their name in that slot. The object of the game is to get as many different signatures as you can.

Sign below if:

You were a cheerleader

_____

You played in the band

_____

You played a high school sport

_____

You have been a coach or manager

_____

You ever worked in a concession stand

_____

You dated an athlete

_____

You have driven more than an hour to go to a football game

_____

You really go to football games because they are social occasions

_____

(Add your own questions for extra fun!)

Football trivia—The following is a fun trivia game, especially for the not-so-avid fan. Pass out football-shaped pieces of paper and ask your guests to number from 1 to 7. Ask them to answer the following questions *true* or *false*. Find out what they know! Answers provided below.

1. In the United States, football is played by two teams with at least eleven players on each team. *(True)*
2. The team with the best-looking jerseys wins. *(False)*
3. The player's name is written on the back of his jersey so the quarterback will know who to throw the ball to. *(False, it is for identification purposes for spectators and officials.)*
4. The Rose Bowl is played in Arizona. *(False, California)*
5. Under their uniforms, football players wear shoulder pads, hip pads, thigh pads, and knee pads. *(True)*
6. The object of the game is to get the ball across the goal line. *(True)*
7. Joe Namath was the football player known for wearing ladies' pantyhose. *(True)*
8. The Downtown Athletic Club in New York City awards the Heisman Trophy to the most outstanding college football player in the nation each year. *(True)*
9. Walter Peyton's nickname was Sugar Daddy. *(False, Sweetness)*
10. All of the plays start with the ball between or on the hash marks. *(True)*

The one with the most answers correct is your Football Trivia winner.

Football charades—Ask an avid football fan to act out the signals that referees use in calling a football game. Many times the signals can also be found on the back of old football programs. Some suggestions are:

Offsides	Clipping
Illegal procedure	Safety
Holding	Touchdown
Face mask	First down
Delay of game	Time out
Roughing the kicker	Roughing the passer
Unsportsmanlike conduct	Intentional grounding

Guests each get a piece of paper and guess the infraction the player is acting out, writing their answers down. The player with the most guesses correct is winner of the game. The prize for the winner might be a referee's whistle.

Devotion

Zig Ziglar says, "Individuals score points, but it takes a team to win the game." Zig is right. You can have a great athlete who can score many points, but if he doesn't have others to block for him and play defense, he will not win the game. Football is a team sport. The best teams are those who play together and realize they cannot do it without each other. When a great team loses, many times it is because not everyone played to their potential.

In the game of life, too, many of us believe we can do it on our own. We have education, we have our life experiences, and there is rarely a problem that comes up that we can't fix. We think we are winning the game of life. What happens when we finally come against something we cannot think our way through or pull enough strings to fix the problem? What will happen when you come to the end of the game of life, and you don't have enough to get you to the next round?

If you have not contemplated these things, today may be a good time to start. There is an answer. It is to play on the team. This team's Head Coach has come to the end of the game and prepared a way for you and me to win the game. He has your spot reserved. All you have to do is realize you can't win the game alone. Ask Him to help you, and join His team. He is the victor, and when the end of your life comes, He is the only way you can win. If you are interested in hearing more about this team and our Coach, I would be glad to talk to you later. Just ask.

Refreshments

The refreshments for this party should resemble things you would serve at a tailgate party.

- Pigs in a blanket
- Cheese dip and chips
- Caramel Dip *(recipe in back)*

Taking It Home

Team schedules for each of your guests would make great take-home favors. Many area businesses make these available. If you cannot find one, make your own. On the back, you could put 2 Timothy 4:7—"I have fought the good fight, I have finished the race, I have kept the faith."

Pumpkin Patch Party

Theme
Fun in the pumpkin patch

A Party For
Elementary-age children

Invitations
Front: *Join us in the Pumpkin Patch . . .*
Inside: *. . . for bunches of fun!*

Date: _____

Time: _____

Place: _____

RSVP: _____

Be sure to bring a pumpkin to decorate!

Decorations
Pumpkins, scarecrows, fall leaves, crows, gourds, hay bales, cornucopia, squash, nuts

Just for Fun

Decorate pumpkins—Have a bag of markers, paint, carving tools, and the like for your guests to use to decorate their pumpkins. You may even want to have hats, costume jewelry, and neckties for the finishing touches.

Pumpkin pal—Have one small baking pumpkin for each child to decorate and take home. These small pumpkins are relatively inexpensive and can be purchased in the produce section of your local grocery store.

Pin the stem on the pumpkin—A fun game for young as well as old. You will need a pumpkin drawn on poster board, one stem per player made from construction paper, tape to attach the stem to the poster board, and a blindfold. The object of the game is to put the stem in the proper place on the pumpkin. The trick is that each player will be blindfolded and spun around several times before they are let loose to pin their stem on the pumpkin. For younger players, you will want to spin them only once or twice. For the more seasoned players you may want to make it more difficult.

Candy corn guess—Prepare this game ahead of time. Fill a jar with candy corn. Count the number of corn pieces in the jar (the jar can be any size). Take a card and write down the number of candy pieces you counted and seal it in an envelope. Give each guest an opportunity to guess the number of candy pieces in the jar. Record their guesses. Later in the party, after each guest has ventured a guess, reveal the correct answer in the envelope. The guest who guessed the closest to the correct answer wins the jar of candy corn.

Pumpkin patch relay— Place in two bags two sets of large adult clothing, such as you would use to dress a scarecrow. Make sure there are at least as many clothing articles as you will have people playing the game. Have your guests divide into two teams and line up in single-file lines. The first player in the row runs down and takes one article of clothing out of the bag. He or she puts it on. Then that person will run back to the line. She hands off her item to the next person in line, who then puts the article of clothing on. That person wearing the first person's article runs down to the sack and gets an article of clothing out of the bag. He puts it on and runs back to the next person in line. This person puts on the first two articles and runs down to get his item out of the bag. He puts it on and runs back to the next person who puts on all the articles already chosen. He then goes to the bag to repeat the same process. The last person to run the relay should be a fully dressed scarecrow. When he retrieves his last article from the bag and puts it on, he calls out "caw caw" (like a crow). This signals the end of the game and the winning team.

The Pumpkin Patch Parable is a book written by Liz Curtis Higgs. It would be a wonderful addition to your party. Your church or public library should have a copy. It can also be ordered at www.LizCurtisHiggs.com. The book is hardcover and will cost around $7.00. You could use this as your devotion part of your party.

Devotion

(This devotion is most effective if done as an object lesson. Prepare ahead of time by having newspaper, a knife, a pumpkin, a candle, a lighter or matches, and a cloth available. You may want to pre-carve the pumpkin to save presentation time.)

(Ask) Does anyone know where pumpkins come from? (Wait for response.) That's right, they are picked from a vine that comes from the ground. When the farmer goes to pick the pumpkin, it is usually dirty and sitting in dirt. Then the farmer picks that pumpkin, brings it home, and washes it. The farmer then cuts the top off of the pumpkin and takes out the mushy, gooey seeds and membrane. He totally cleans the pumpkin out (cut open the pumpkin as you say this and clean out the insides). Then he takes a knife and carves the pumpkin into the shape and style he wants it to be (carve your pumpkin). The farmer then puts a candle on the inside of the pumpkin, and anyone walking by can see the light shining through the shapes cut by the farmer.

In a funny way, we are like this pumpkin. God is the farmer. God planted you in your mother's womb even before you were born. Psalm 139:13–14 says, "For you created my inmost being; you knit me together in my mother's womb. I praise you because I am fearfully and wonderfully made." We grow up in the dirt of the world around us, and one day God says, "I choose you." If you will allow Him, He will take away the wrong things you have done. Just as the farmer cleans all of the yuck out of the inside of the pumpkin, God can and will clean you and me up on the inside, too. He carves us into usable vessels just like we carved out the pumpkin. Then He puts His light in us so that we can shine the light of God just like the pumpkin shines the light of the candle that is inside. Then others will be able to see God's light because we have it in us. We can't do all this on our own. We must have the Farmer, God, to pick us, clean us up, carve us into usable vessels, then put His light in us. If you are interested in asking God to do this in your life, I would love to talk to you later.

Refreshments

 Pumpkin Dip *(recipe in back)*

 Pumpkin Bread *(recipe in back)*

Taking It Home

Roasted nuts in a bag would be a great take-home gift. Attach a small note that says, "You are special." A slight twist on this could be to roast pumpkin seeds or pecans and put them in bags. If you use the Pumpkin Pals activity, these can be taken home as a favor as well.

Hunters Brunch

Theme
Prayer

A Party For
Women whose husbands have gone hunting

Invitations
Has "Buck Fever" invaded your home?
Come join us for brunch as we pray for those affected.

Date: _____

Time: _____

Place: _____

RSVP: _____

Decorations
Camouflage, hunting equipment and apparel, deer and other animals

Just for Fun

Hunting wreath—A fun thing to do at the hunters brunch is to make a hunting wreath. Ask each guest to bring a grapevine wreath to be decorated at the party. Let your guests know what they will be making and ask them to bring along items for the wreath. The hostess will want to have some of the following items:

florist wire
camouflage ribbon
pine cones
hot glue
Spanish moss
sweet gum balls
acorns
old cypress knees
drift wood
turkey or duck feathers
antlers
duck call
duck decoy
spent shells
small children's toys, like a pick-up truck, bow and arrow, or a four wheeler

You can use anything on the wreath that makes you think of hunting. At the party, have a wonderful time as you create hunting wreaths.

Ladies' hunting expedition to the mall—After brunch, go to a favorite shopping spot and hunt for bargains.

Devotion

Did your husband leave this morning whispering this prayer?

As I rise before the sun,
I pray for warmth and lots of fun.
If I should find that great big deer,
Help me kill it so I can cheer.
But if it doesn't come my way,
Keep me ready for another day.

Or maybe this was your prayer:

As I lay here in my warm bed,
Help him remember what I said:
If he should kill a big ol' buck,
Help him get it to the truck.
May it not have horns so tall,
So it won't be mounted and hung on my wall.

This morning we have gathered together to enjoy some fun and friendship. I am so glad you came. The guys are probably having a wonderful time, and I wanted us to get together and have a good time, too. Hunting season can be a difficult time if your husband is the kind who gets "buck fever" and all he thinks about is being in the woods. I have asked _____ to share a testimony about how she handles this difficult season of the year. *(Arrange beforehand for a woman to give a testimony about how she handles hunting season. Her major thrust should be that she prays and asks God to give her patience and a sweet spirit. Give some suggestions of ways she goes on with life or talks to her husband about feeling like she is carrying more responsibility. She could also suggest some fun things the ladies could do together to not feel left out.)*

I would like for us to spend a few minutes praying for our families as they are out hunting. If it is okay, we will start by having a few minutes of quiet prayer where you may want to confess any sin. Then I have asked a couple of ladies to pray aloud. _____ will pray for

71

the safety of our hunters, _____ will pray for us that we will have a good attitude, and I will pray that our husbands will keep their eyes open to see the needs of those around them, and that they will grow spiritually during their time in the quiet of nature.

Refreshments
- Breakfast casserole
- Cheese Grits *(recipe in back)*
- Biscuits

Taking It Home

Hunter's wife survival kit: Kleenex for those down days, popcorn to be enjoyed with a chick flick, ear plugs so he doesn't wake you in the mornings, a rubber band so you can remember to be flexible, and a copy of the Hunter's Prayer and Hunter's Wife's Prayer (as read in the devotion) on a small piece of paper rolled and tied with a camouflage bow.

Checkered Flag

Theme
Evangelism

A Party For
Racing fans and their families

Invitations
Racers start your engines,
Bring your pit crew, and
Speed over to our house to see
Who will take the checkered flag!

Date: _____

Time: _____

Place: _____

RSVP: _____

Decorations
Checkered flags, NASCAR stuff, matchbox cars, racing
paraphernalia

Just for Fun

Remote control car races—Have a couple of remote control cars, or ask guests to bring their own remote control cars. Map out a racecourse and let the fun begin. Racers of all ages will have fun!

Fan dress contest—Let guests know ahead of time that you would like for them to participate in the best-dressed fan contest. Let them know that prizes will be given in several categories. Some of the winners could be the most creative, the most outlandish, the most serious, and the most crew spirit. Create your own categories. Let all of your guests know they are winners just for participating. Prizes for this event could be matchbox cars or other NASCAR collectibles.

Devotion

We all know that the objective in racing is to be the driver who takes the checkered flag. We also know that it takes much preparation, planning, and practice to become the one in the winner's circle. The racing team makes sure the car is functioning as close to perfection as possible. Extra parts are prepared in case of an emergency, and fresh tires and gasoline are readied. A plan of action is prepared so that the crew can be ready on specific laps for pit stops that must be carried out in seconds. Practice laps are taken so that everyone is prepared for the big event. When it comes to race time, the driver himself must be prepared physically, mentally, and spiritually. Every driver who sits behind the steering wheel feeling the motor of his car racing at speeds exceeding 150 miles per hour knows any minute could be his last, so he must be prepared in case he "hits the wall."

In 2001, one of racing's legends found out how true this was. Dale Earnhardt started the race like every other driver, thinking today would be his day to take the checkered flag. Dale did take a checkered flag that day. It was not the checkered flag made by human hands. Dale had prepared for this race years before when he asked Jesus to forgive him of his sins and come into his heart. The driver called "The Intimidator" wasn't perfect after that experience, but he knew he could ask for forgiveness when he messed up, and God would forgive him. Dale knew that when life ended he would go to heaven and win the ultimate race, the race of life. When it comes to the race of life, it doesn't matter how many races you have won here on earth, or that you are a legend in the eyes of men. All that matters is when you "hit the wall" you have prepared for the final race by asking Christ into your heart. If you would like to know more about how you can finish well in the race of life, I would like to talk to you about it later.

Refreshments

- Pretzels
- Popcorn
- Hot wings
- Hot dogs
- Chips
- Root beer

Taking It Home

Small checkered flags with "Finish Well" written on them
Matchbox car with the "Finish Well" message attached

Holiday Parties

The Time Has Come
(New Year's Eve)

Theme
New Year's Eve—It's time for a new start.

A Party For
Youth or adults

Invitations
The invitations for this party could be anything having to do with time. Our suggestion is:

Front: *The time has come . . .*
Inside: *To celebrate a New Year!*
Come join the fun.

Date: _____
Time: _____
Place: _____
RSVP: _____

Decorations

Clocks, balloons, confetti, hourglasses, calendars, party blowers, party hats, streamers. Anything that reminds you that time is passing and a new year is dawning would be perfect for this occasion. You can let your imagination go wild on this one. If you have a grandfather clock, you could make it a focal point to help mark the hours passing, and to help celebrate the arrival of the New Year in "grand" fashion.

Just for Fun

Time charades—Act out the following and see if your team can guess your phrases about "time."

Just passing time	Father Time
Time flies when you're having fun	Time line
	Tool Time
A stitch in time saves nine	(from the TV series
Just in the nick of time	Home Improvement)
Time out	New York Times
Time to run	Times Square
Bedtime	Timeless tradition
Time's up	Somewhere in time
Time travel	Once upon a time . . .

A year of significance—Have guests divide into two teams and have them list the most significant events of the last year. The team that comes up with the most events wins. Invite a friend who has had a challenging or victorious last year to share his or her testimony. People respond well to stories.

Devotion

What do you think of when someone says "Happy New Year"? Many think of parties, Dick Clark and the ball dropping in Times Square, New Year resolutions . . . or if you're like me, you think of an opportunity to start over. There are new possibilities, a new calendar of 365 new days, challenges, and victories that await. We can leave behind the things we have messed up. The time has come to set new goals. A new beginning may be the incentive we've needed to push ahead toward former goals that were set but were left behind or never even attempted. When I think of starting over and having a new start, 2 Corinthians 5:17 comes to my mind. It says, "If anyone is in Christ, he is a new creation; the old has gone, the new has come!" In my life I came to a point where I realized the time had come for a new start. Though I was not an axe murderer or convicted felon, I knew that I had done things that were wrong in God's eyes. I knew I felt guilt when I did them. I asked God to forgive me and give me that new start that the verse described. I told Him that if He would take away my sin, I would try to do what would please Him the rest of my days. I wish I could tell you I never mess up now, but that would not be true. However, I do know that I can go back to God when I make poor choices and He will forgive me. As I look at the New Year, one of my goals is to read God's Word daily and to find out what He wants me to do. I am sure you have goals you have been thinking about, too.

I have some stationery and envelopes for each of us. I would like for us to take a minute to write down three goals we would like to work on this year. Seal your envelope when you are finished and address the envelope to yourself. In a few months I plan to send your envelope back to you in the mail. This will be a good reminder of our goals and will help us to evaluate how we are progressing toward their completion. If you would like to know more about how you can start this New Year with a clean slate with God, I would be glad to talk to you about it later. Please ask me.

Refreshments

Your refreshments for this party will be determined by the length of the party and what time you choose to begin. If you are starting early in the evening, plan for heavy snacks or a light meal. The later you start, the lighter you can go. If you are starting after 10:00 P.M., you may want to even think about serving breakfast foods. The following are some ideas.

- Jambalaya *(recipe in back)*
- Holiday Cheese Ball *(recipe in back)*
- Fiesta Tamale Dip *(recipe in back)*
- Cheese Grits *(recipe in back)*
- Mini Biscuits *(recipe in back)*

Taking It Home

Clock pins: You may provide your guests with clocks to wear. The clock pins could be used as mementos of the fun occasion. These can be made by using a canning lid and gluing a paper face of a clock to the lid. Add a pin to the back, and your friends will have a reminder of the fun you had as you all watched time fly. Remind your guests that each minute is a gift from God.

Blessing Box: Empty a small matchbox. Write out a blessing or prayer to be placed inside the box. Wrap boxes with gold wrap and include a gift tag that says, "The year ahead is a gift to you." A possible prayer could be the prayer of Jabez from 1 Chronicles 4:10: "Oh, that you would bless me indeed and enlarge my territory! Let your hand be with me, and keep me from harm so that I will be free from pain." Another prayer could be, "The LORD bless you and keep you; the LORD make his face shine upon you and be gracious to you; the LORD turn his face toward you and give you peace" (Numbers 6:24–26).

Goals letter: If you encourage your guests to set goals, be sure to mail them back in a few months. That will be a wonderful reminder of any decision that was made at the party and of all of the fun everyone enjoyed.

Celebrate the King
(January 8)

Theme
Evangelism

A Party For
Youth or adult Elvis fans!

Invitations
What do peanut butter and banana sandwiches,
Memphis, Tennessee, and a birthday cake
all have in common?
If you guessed Elvis Presley's birthday,
you would be right!
Come help us celebrate.

Date: _____

Time: _____

Place: _____

RSVP: _____

Decorations

Elvis memorabilia, guitars, rhinestones, animal print material, old record player, old albums, movies, pictures

Just for Fun

Elvis trivia game—Copy out the following questions and see how many of your guests know the answers.

When or where did Elvis marry Priscilla? *May 1, 1967, in Las Vegas, Nevada*

Elvis' daughter was born February 1, 1968. What was her name? *Lisa Marie*

In November 1958, in what branch of service did Elvis enlist? *The army, in Ft. Hood Texas*

What country was Elvis sent to? *Germany*

What was his rank? *Sergeant*

What was Elvis' mother's name? *Gladys*

His first single was released in 1954; what was the song? *That's Alright, Mama*

What Elvis movie was made in New Orleans? *King Creole*

In 1967 Elvis purchased a home in Memphis. What is the name of that home? *Graceland*

What year did Elvis die? *1977*

Pin the scarf on Elvis—For this game you will need a picture or poster of Elvis, a blindfold, and a scarf with tape. Blindfold your guests one at a time, spin them around a time or two, and have them try to pin the scarf on the King.

Shake, rattle, and roll charades—Play charades using the following Elvis song titles. You can divide into teams or just have guests draw a song title from a basket and see if the other guests can guess the title he or she is acting out.

Love Me Tender	All Shook Up
Spinout	Heartbreak Hotel
Loving You	Blue Christmas
Jailhouse Rock	Don't Be Cruel
Hound Dog	It's Now or Never
Can't Help Falling in Love	Stuck on You
Blue Suede Shoes	Are You Lonesome Tonight?

Devotion

January 8, 1935, marked the beginning of an era. Elvis Aaron Presley was born into the home of a poor, hard-working, humble family in Tupelo, Mississippi. This child born in obscurity was destined for greatness as the King of Rock and Roll. The dark-haired, handsome, leg-twitching vocalist became the heartthrob of the nation's youth. His spine-tingling renditions of *Loving You*, *Love Me Tender*, *Jailhouse Rock*, and *Hound Dog* made the youth of his day crown him the King. Elvis was generous and kind to his family and friends. Even those who didn't appreciate his music and movies respected his generosity.

There was another boy born in obscurity to poor, hardworking, humble parents. Though many did not recognize Him as such, He truly was the King. He never recorded an album, He never made a movie, but what He did was to live a perfect life and take on all the sin of mankind so we could find forgiveness from the Creator.

Elvis learned at his mother's knee about the one true King, whose name was Jesus. Elvis loved to sing praises to this King. Elvis wasn't perfect, but he found forgiveness, just as we can, at the foot of the King's cross.

Today we celebrate the birthday of Elvis. I enjoy listening to his music and watching his movies, but the King I really want to celebrate today is King Jesus. None can *Love Me as Tender* as Jesus. Nothing can *Shake, Rattle, and Roll* me as long as I put my trust in Him. There will never be a time when Jesus will not be *Loving You* and me. If you have not met the King, I would love to introduce you.

"I'm not a King, Christ is King. I'm just an entertainer."
—Elvis Presley

Refreshments
⊘ Peanut butter and banana sandwiches
⊘ King cake
⊘ Hot dogs (hound dogs)

Taking It Home
Sunglasses that are glittered and a note that reads, "My King Lives!"

Mardi Gras Madness

Purpose
Spiritual growth

A Party For
Youth or adults

Invitations
It's Mardi Gras fun planned
For all of the crew,
The food is cooking
And we're waiting for you.

Date: _____

Time: _____

Place: _____

RSVP: _____

Decorations

Beads, coins (doubloons), masks, umbrellas, jazz instruments, feathers, balloons, anything purple, gold, or green, crepe paper streamers, sequins, confetti

Just for Fun

Creole cookies—This is a fun game that can be played with any number of guests. Divide your guests into equal groups. Explain to the teams that the object of the game is to make cookies. Give them all of the ingredients they will need to make a batch of cookies (i.e. flour, sugar, brown sugar, butter, eggs, salt, baking soda, vanilla, chocolate chips, oatmeal). Each team is given a bowl and a spatula, but no measuring devices or recipe. Have oven preheated to 350 degrees. Have a judge taste each batch and determine a Creole cookie winner.

Secret identity—This game is meant to be silly, but it will also give you the opportunity to know your guests better. Your guests take turns being the Story Teller. The Teller draws a name from the secret identity basket. Inside this basket you will have the names of famous people (i.e. Regis Philbin, Dr. Phil, Mike Tyson, Mr. Rogers, Madonna). The Teller is to tell about a specific event from their own life using the dialect and persona of the character they drew. The Teller can tell about one of the following events: an embarrassing situation, their best vacation, a perfect day (made up of course), a great hunting story or fisherman's tale, or a practical joke. After the Teller has completed his/her story, the group tries to guess who the secret identity was.

Paper plate masks—Take paper plates and cut them in half. Punch a small hole on either side to thread ribbon through to tie on the mask when complete. Cut out two eyeholes and an indention for the nose from the bottom of the plate. Have sequins, feathers, glue, glitter, beads, and other items available to decorate the masks.

Devotion

We have had fun this evening creating beautiful, fun masks. Masks were used in early civilizations as a part of theatrical productions. By changing his mask, one actor could play many parts. He could be both hero and villain, depending on the mask that he wore at the time. We do not wear theatrical masks in our everyday lives, but many of us do change our persona depending on who we are with or where we are. If we are with our friends who enjoy worldly living, we change to fit in with the crowd. If we are with our church friends, we change to be like them.

A young lady named Mia said, "I felt like a chameleon because I never knew who I really was. I would come to the end of the day and just feel so empty." Mia's words may describe you or me. There is someone who knows you even better than you know yourself. Listen to Psalm 139:1–3: "O Lord, you have searched me and you know me. You know when I sit and when I rise; you perceive my thoughts from afar. You discern my going out and my lying down; you are familiar with all my ways."

God does know the real you. He is not fooled by the masks we put on to fool other people. Today God wants you to know He loves the real you. Psalm 139 goes on to say, "Search me, O God, and know my heart; test me and know my anxious thoughts. See if there is any offensive way in me, and lead me in the way everlasting" (Psalm 139:23–24). God wants each of us to be who He created us to be. He wants to daily have time with us and to tell us how precious we are to Him.

There is an old song that you may have heard. The words say, "Just as I am, without one plea, but that Thy blood was shed for me, and that Thou bidst me come to Thee, O Lamb of God, I come, I come." Today, God wants to take away your emptiness and give you abundant life in Him. The way to do that is to unmask yourself and come to Him just as you are. If you would like to talk to me further about how to have a more abundant life with Christ, I would be glad to talk to you.

Refreshments

- Red beans and rice
- Jambalaya *(recipe in back)*
- King Cake (a coffee cake served in New Orleans during Mardi Gras)

Taking It Home

The masks made in the **Just for Fun** activity are for each guest to take home. You might want to send home a card with the mask that says, "God looks behind the mask and loves the real you."

Eggstra Special Easter

Theme
Jesus makes Easter eggstra special.

A Party For
Elementary-age children

Invitations
If you are planning to hand-deliver them, consider putting your invitation inside a plastic Easter egg. If you are planning to mail your them, use Easter eggs made from construction paper and decorated by children.

> **Front:** *Come join us*
> **Inside:** *For an eggstra special egg hunt*
>
> *Date:* _____
> *Time:* _____
> *Place:* _____
> *RSVP:* _____

Please bring a basket and a dozen plastic eggs.

Decorations

The decorations for this party can be anything having to do with Easter. Put the cross and Christian symbols in a prominent place. Tie the traditional decorations, like the eggs, to Christian themes. For example: If you have a basket of eggs, why not have a small sign that says, "I've put all of my eggs in one basket and given them to the Lord." Another way to tie in Christian themes may be to use verses of Scripture or spiritual sayings on small cards. An example of this may be to place a sign beside a grouping of bunnies that says "Creatures great or small, God created them all."

Just for Fun

Eggstra special egg hunt will be lots of fun. The eggstra special eggs will be eggs that will later be used in the devotion part of the party. There will be twelve special eggs that should be numbered 1 to 12 and filled with the contents listed below. Put the special eggs in with the eggs your guests have brought for a wonderful egg hunt. At the end of the hunt, you may want to have a special gift or prize for those who turn in a special egg. Collect the special eggs in a basket to be used in the devotion portion of the party.

Decorating blown eggs—Depending on the ages of your guests, you may want to have the eggs blown before the party. To blow the eggs, take raw eggs and pierce the ends with a pin or sharp object. Your holes will need to be big enough for air to force the yolk through. Then blow the egg yolk out. Children can then decorate the eggs using markers or paint. Again, take the age of your guests into consideration as you make these plans. You may also need adult supervision.

Creative cupcakes can be made at snack time. Prepare cupcakes ahead of time and have icing, green-colored coconut for grass, jellybeans for eggs, and other items available for decorating the cupcakes that are edible and fun to decorate with.

Devotion

The devotion for this party is to tell the Easter story using the Eggstra Special Eggs. You can buy devotional egg kits like our Eggstra Special Eggs in Christian bookstores, or you can make your own using the directions below.

You will need twelve plastic Easter eggs, the items listed below, Bible verses on separate slips of paper, tape to seal the eggs shut, and a permanent marker to number your special eggs.

Egg 1: A perfumed card—Mark 14:8.
Egg 2: Small portion of cracker—Mark 14:22–25
Egg 3: Paper with "Abba, Father" written on it
—Mark 14:36
Egg 4: Three dimes—Matthew 27:3
Egg 5: Feather—Mark 14:72
Egg 6: Purple fabric or thorn vine—Mark 15:17–18
Egg 7: Small nail—Mark 15:25
Egg 8: White cloth—Mark 15:46
Egg 9: Cinnamon stick or cloves—Mark 16:1
Egg 10: Rock—Mark 16:4
Egg 11: Empty—Mark 16:6
Egg 12: Cotton ball—Mark 16:19

Scriptures for the Eggstra Special Eggs

Mark 14:8—"She did what she could. She poured perfume on my body beforehand to prepare for my burial."

Mark 14:22–25—"While they were eating, Jesus took bread, gave thanks and broke it, and gave it to his disciples, saying, 'Take it; this is my body.'"

Mark 14:36—"'*Abba*, Father,' he said, 'everything is possible for you. Take this cup from me. Yet not what I will, but what you will.'"

Matthew 27:3—"When Judas, who had betrayed him, saw that Jesus was condemned, he was seized with remorse and returned the thirty silver coins to the chief priests and the elders."

Mark 14:72—"Immediately the rooster crowed the second time. Then Peter remembered the word Jesus had spoken to him: 'Before the rooster crows twice you will disown me three times.' And he broke down and wept."

Mark 15:17–18—"They put a purple robe on Him, then twisted together a crown of thorns and set it on him. And they began to call out to him, 'Hail, King of the Jews!'"

Mark 15:25—"It was the third hour when they crucified him."

Mark 15:46—"So Joseph bought some linen cloth, took down the body, wrapped it in the linen, and placed it in a tomb cut out of rock. Then he rolled a stone against the entrance of the tomb."

Mark 16:1—"When the Sabbath was over, Mary Magdalene, Mary the mother of James, and Salome brought spices so that they might go to anoint Jesus' body."

Mark 16:4—"But when they looked up, they saw that the stone, which was very large, had been rolled away."

Mark 16:6—"'Don't be alarmed,' he said. 'You are looking for Jesus the Nazarene, who was crucified. He has risen! He is not here. See the place where they laid him.'"

Mark 16:19— "After the Lord Jesus had spoken to them, he was taken up into heaven and he sat at the right hand of God."

To tell the Easter story to your guests, open each egg in order, one at a time. The numbers will help you keep them in order and give you the verses you will need. Ask guests to read the verses at the appropriate time in the story. Your storytime might go something like this:

Today I would like to use our Eggstra Special Eggs to help me tell a story. I may need some help from my friends.

Egg 1. (*Open*) Our story is about a man named Jesus. He was a man who never did anything wrong. He was God's Son. He came to save the world by giving His life. Our first egg has a card in it. I would like for you to smell this card. (***Pass it around.***) This card reminds me of something special a lady did for Jesus. _____, would you read Mark 14:8? Jesus knew that He would have to die so that we could have forgiveness of the wrong things we do. He was perfect and was the only one who could pay for our wrong. This lady used some expensive, sweet-smelling perfume to anoint Jesus to prepare Him for burial.

Egg 2. Jesus wanted to eat one more time with His friends. They had a special meal. A part of that meal included eating some bread. Jesus told them something special. _____, would you read what Jesus said in Mark 14:22–25? Every time the friends would get together from then on to eat, they were to remember what Jesus did for them.

Egg 3. After they ate supper, Jesus went away to pray. He knew difficult times were ahead. _____, would you read Mark 14:36?

Egg 4. As soon as Jesus finished praying, some guards took Jesus away to kill Him. Judas, one of Jesus' followers, had told the guards where to find Jesus. Later he was very sorry he had done this. _____, would you read Matt 27:3?

Egg 5. Judas was not the only one of Jesus' followers who did something he should not. Peter, one of Jesus' friends, was afraid of the people, and when they asked him if he was Jesus' friend, he said no. Jesus had told Peter that he would say he did not know Jesus three times before a rooster crowed. Peter loved Jesus and could not imagine that happening. But when Peter got scared, he did just what Jesus said he would do. _____, would you read Mark 14:72? This feather represents the rooster that crowed.

Egg 6. Jesus was being questioned by the leaders, who were saying, "Are you God's Son?" Jesus answered that He was, and the guards and leaders got very angry. They put a purple robe and a crown of thorns on Jesus because they were mocking Him and saying He was not really God's Son. _____, would you read Mark 15:17–18 to us?

Egg 7. Soldiers took Jesus to a cross and nailed His hands and feet to that cross. _____, would you read Mark 15:25?

Egg 8. It was a sad time. Jesus died on that cross though He had done nothing wrong. He died to pay for the wrong things that we would do. Another word for our wrongdoing is sin. Jesus paid for our sins. Joseph of Arimathea came and took Jesus down from the cross and put Him in a cave to bury Him. _____, would you read Mark 15:46? In those days they would wrap the dead in cloth and put them in a cave and seal the cave with a large rock. They would put spices in the cloth to make the body smell better.

Egg 9. The spices might have smelled something like this. _____, would you read Mark 16:1?

Egg 10. These ladies came to put the spices on Jesus' body two days after He had died. When they got there, the big stone that was used to keep animals out had been rolled away from the opening of the grave. _____, would you read Mark 16:4?

Egg 11. When the ladies looked inside, they were upset because Jesus wasn't there. They thought maybe someone had stolen His body. An angel assured them that Jesus had not been stolen, but that He had risen, or come back from being dead. _____, would you read Mark 16:6? Jesus had told His followers that He would die and then come back from the grave. His followers knew that was impossible for a man to do. But God's Son could and did do just that. With God, all things are possible. Jesus paid for our sin by dying on the cross, and God gave Jesus new life by raising Him from the dead. God can give you new life, too. If we believe Jesus was God's Son, that He died to pay for our wrongdoings, that He can and will forgive us if we ask, we too can live forever with Jesus. Jesus' friends saw Jesus here on earth for forty days after He had been raised from the dead. Mark 16:19 tells us what happened next. _____, will you read that for us?

Egg 12. I have put a cotton ball in this egg because it reminds me of the clouds. God took Jesus up into heaven. He probably disappeared from His followers' sight up into the clouds. In John 14:3 Jesus told His followers, "And if I go and prepare a place for you, I will come back and take you to be with me that you also may be where I am." That is what Easter is all about. Jesus lived a perfect life, died, was buried, rose from the dead, and right now is in heaven just waiting for those who choose Him. If you would like to know more about how you can choose Jesus, please talk to me later.

Refreshments
- Resurrection Cookies *(recipe in back)*
- Creative cupcakes
- Party Punch *(recipe in back)*

Taking It Home
Eggstra special egg kits, with the 12 eggs and Scriptures, can be prepared for each family. Prepare these ahead of time and give them to your guests to be used for years to come. Be sure to insert the verse strip inside each egg.

Blown eggs allow children to take home the eggs they created.

Patriotic Picnic

Theme
Celebrate American independence, patriotism, and freedom.

A Party For
Adults, children, youth or families

Invitations
Front: *Put on your red, white, and blue . . .*
Inside: *And join us for a patriotic picnic*

Date: _____
Time: _____
Place: _____
RSVP: _____
What to bring: _____

Decorations

The possibilities are limitless in decorating for this fun event. Your main colors will be red, white, and blue. However, with the picnic theme, you can also pick up the picnic motif: red or blue gingham cloth, streamers, flags, baskets, fireworks, metal washtub (with ice & drinks), confetti, Melon Basket (see recipe), fresh fruit, fresh flowers (daisies).

Just for Fun

Outdoor games are a given for this event: horseshoes, volleyball, wiffle ball, tether ball, badminton, swimming, egg toss, water balloon toss, hula-hoop contest, water balloon fight, capture the flag.

American Presidents—A game where you hand out paper and pencils and have your guests name as many American Presidents as they can in three minutes. (Your older guests will have a real advantage.)

Relay Play—Divide your guests into teams and have a relay contest.

Pledge relay: Have the first person in line run to a designated spot and recite the Pledge of Allegiance. When the person has completed his or her recitation, have him or her run back to the team and tag the next person in line, who repeats the relay until all members on your team have had a turn.

Yankee Doodle relay: The first person in line gallops to a designated spot, picks up a feather, sticks it behind his ear, and calls out "macaroni," then puts the feather back down and gallops back to the next person in line, who repeats the relay. Continue until one team wins.

Paul Revere relay: The first person in line hollers out, "The British are coming!" The next person hollers, "The British are coming!" and so on until every one in line has repeated the phrase. The first person then runs to the end of the line and the person who was second in line yells the phrase again until once again everyone in the line has repeated the refrain. Then the first person again runs to the end of the line and the next person repeats the phrase and then the rest of the line repeats the phrase one at a time down the line. The winning team is the one who goes all through the line with every person being the leader once and the phrase going through the entire line the last time.

Patriotic Pictionary—Divide your guests into two teams. Have markers and sketching paper available. One team member from each team will be the draw-er. The game judge will choose a piece of paper from the basket that tells the draw-ers what they must depict. The object of the game is to get your team to guess what you are drawing before the other team does. The team that guesses correctly first wins the point. Some suggestions:

The White House
Abraham Lincoln
The Capitol
Betsy Ross
The Star-Spangled Banner
George Washington
The Liberty Bell
Bald Eagle
The U.S. Flag
The Declaration of Independence
The Boston Tea Party
The Lincoln Memorial
Air Force One
God Bless America

Yankee Doodle
The West Wing
The Oval Office
Baseball, hotdogs, apple pie, and Chevrolet
The Statue of Liberty

Devotion

Do you remember where you were September 11, 2001, when terrorists attacked our nation? How did you feel? How has that event changed your life? Many in the United States of America have felt safe for so long that we have forgotten the price that was paid for our freedom. The events of September 11 have helped us remember that freedom comes at a high price. Family after family has been informed of the death of their son, daughter, wife, husband, father, or mother, and we are reminded that liberty comes with a high price tag. I would like for us to take a moment just to say a prayer for those who have lost loved ones and for those who even now represent us by serving in our armed forces. (Arrange ahead of time for someone to pray at this time.)

Another of the things that September 11 makes me think of is that a long time ago someone paid a price so that I could have freedom from the fear of death. His name was Jesus. He is God's Son, and He came as a perfect man to pay the price for my sin. Sin is anything I do that is not what God wants me to do. Jesus knew I could never pay that price because I was not perfect. He chose to die as a payment for the sins of mankind. Galatians 5:1 says, "It is for freedom that Christ has set us free." If you ask Him to forgive your sins and come into your heart, you too may experience this freedom. As we celebrate our freedom today as a country, please keep in mind that there is spiritual freedom available to you also. If you would like to know more about how you can have this freedom from fear, I would be glad to talk to you later.

Refreshments

- Melon Basket *(recipe in back)*
- Patriotic Trifle *(recipe in back)*
- Cookout foods

Taking It Home

Small flag: These are fairly inexpensive at your neighborhood dollar store. Attach a small gift card that says, "Celebrate Your Freedom!" On the back you could print John 3:16.

Gold medal party favors: These can be purchased at Wal-Mart or any party store in the party favors area. Or you could make your own awards. Take a milk cap, wrap it in gold or silver wrapping, and attach a red, white, and blue ribbon. You could even have your own awards ceremony complete with the national anthem and recognition for fun awards. Possibilities might include: best team spirit, best try, most potential, hidden potential, most fun, most Christ-like, great effort, future artist, a Yankee Doodle Dandy, a true patriot, or any other fun award that might apply.

Thanks-Giving Party

Theme
Giving thanks

A Party For
Adults or youth

Invitations
Front: *When I think of all of the things*
I am thankful for . . .
Inside: *. . . you are on the list!*
Come celebrate the season with me.

Your invitation might include this list: God, Family, Friends . . .

Date: _____
Time: _____
Place: _____
RSVP: _____

P.S. Please bring a canned good for our blessing basket.

Decorations

Cornucopia, squash, pumpkins, nuts, gourds, Indian corn, apples, scarecrows, Nuttivity, pilgrims, Indians, turkeys. Anything with a fall or Thanksgiving feel to it would be great for this party.

Just for Fun

A Basket of Blessing is a basket that will be filled with canned goods to be sent to a needy family or organization in your community. Let your guests know ahead of time what they should bring. Your basket could be fixings for a Thanksgiving feast, or you could choose to collect items to be used to fix soup or stew.

A Nuttivity is a craft project that is made by using three green peanuts of varying size, Spanish moss for the bedding, and a piece of cardboard cut to 3x4 inches. Take a pin and make a pea-size hole in each peanut. That will be the face. Glue the moss on the cardboard piece, covering the top surface. Then hot glue your peanuts with the tallest two standing up and the smallest lying on the bed of moss. It should look like Mary, Joseph, and Baby Jesus. Nuttivities are a fun way to help your guests know that you are thankful for Jesus. As they prepare to celebrate Christmas, hopefully they will be able to share the nuttivity with others and tell them about Jesus.

Thankful in Everything is an activity that will give your guests the opportunity to look over the last year and count their many blessings. Each guest will need a piece of paper and something to write with. Start by reading 1 Thessalonians 5:18— "Give thanks in all circumstances, for this is God's will for you in Christ Jesus." Then ask your guests to respond to the following questions by writing out their response on the paper they were given.

What was the best thing that happened to you this year?
What was the worst thing that happened to you this year?
What was something that brought you joy?
What was something that brought you laughter?
What was something that cost you greatly?
What was a simple pleasure?
What made you want to sing?
What made you want to cry?
What have you learned?
What or who have you treasured?

We truly have much to be grateful for. You may want to see if anyone wants to share what he or she wrote for one of the questions. This is a great way to really get to know your guests. If no one wants to answer, you may want to start by sharing your answer to a question or two. They want to get to know you, too.

Devotion

Before the party begins, gather a basket of about 8 to 10 things you are thankful for. These items might include pictures of family, friends, vacations, or business. You may include food, drinks, makeup, your favorite shirt, medicine, bubble bath, or anything God brings to your mind. Be sure you have your Bible in there as well. Begin your presentation by affirming the things your friends have said they were thankful for in the "Thankful in Everything" activity. Bring out your basket and the items one by one, telling your friends what you are thankful for. Save the Bible for last.

When you bring it out, tell them you are thankful for God's Word, which directs you each day. Open the Bible to 1 Thessalonians 5:16–18 and read the verses. The Bible instructs us to "Be joyful always; pray continually; give thanks in all circumstances, for this is God's will for you in Christ Jesus." Notice that it said in *all* circumstances.

Sometimes that can be hard to do. Share a time from your life when you had to go through a difficult circumstance. Acknowledge your struggles, but remind your friends that you were not alone and Jesus was there to help you through it.

Say, "If any of you are interested in knowing how you can have Jesus there with you in the good and bad times of life, I would love to talk to you later." Close by giving your guests a note card and envelope. Challenge them to take the card home with them and write a note to someone who means a lot to them, thanking that person for the contribution he or she has made to their life.

Refreshments

- Chili Stack Ups *(recipe in back)*
- Roll-Ups *(recipe in back)*
- Sweet Treat *(recipe in back)*
- Party Punch *(recipe in back)*

Taking It Home

Stationery with stamped envelope: This is the continuation of your devotion time. With a stamped envelope, they are more likely to mail their note.

Nuttivity: Encourage them to take their nuttivity home and share its message with others.

Miracle on 34th Street
Movie Screening

Theme
Share the miracle that took place in your life.

A Party For
Youth or adults

Invitations
Have the invitation in the shape or style of a movie ticket.

Front: *You are invited to a private screening of . . .*
Inside: *Miracle on 34th Street*

Date: _____

Time: _____

Place: _____

RSVP: _____

Decorations

This is the easiest party to decorate for. Use all of your normal Christmas decor. If you have already decorated for the holidays, there is little extra work. If you haven't already decorated, this is a wonderful excuse to do so. You will be able to enjoy the product of your labor for weeks. If you choose to do this party in a month other than December, you may not want to go all out, but these are some things we would suggest:

Signs that say, "I believe," or "Santa stops here"
Candy canes
Pin that says, "I believe in miracles"
Small tree

Just for Fun

Your main event will be the movie. Because of the length of the movie, you will not want to plan many other activities.

Autograph session—The idea is to get as many different signatures as you can. The only catch is that the questions must be answered honestly. This is a great get-to-know-you game and can be started as soon as guests begin to arrive. It will give guests who may not know each other the opportunity to find out about each other.

Sign below if . . .
You wait to shop until December 24th.

_____

You look forward to the day the kids go back to school.

_____

You are sneaky and open your presents before Christmas.

_____

Your favorite song is "Jingle Bells."

_____

You have finished all your shopping.

_____

You like fruitcake.

_____

You have eaten turkey at least three times this holiday season. _____
You still believe in Santa.

_____

Door prizes can be given at the beginning, end, or in the middle of the movie, or at each of these times. If you give them at the end, it will encourage your guests to stay. You will also want to start the movie as soon as most of your guests have arrived. Being on time wins points. Have your guests sign up for door prizes as they enter your home. Have some paper, a pen, and a basket of some type to put the names in. Some possible suggestions for door prizes might be:

- Santa on a sleigh figurine—the movie's opening scene
- Candy cane—the movie's closing scene
- Dream-home catalog—where the little girl gets her request
- "I believe" button
- Movie passes for a local theatre
- Gift card from a local movie rental place

Devotion

(You may want to have an intermission in the middle of the movie and use it as your devotion time as well as give a door prize or two. That way anyone who is late or must leave early won't miss the most important part.)

We are here tonight to watch the movie *Miracle on 34th Street*. We will continue with the movie momentarily, but I want to take a minute and share with you the greatest miracle that ever took place in my life. It was when I realized

I did wrong and did things that did not please God. I knew I would have to answer for those wrong things. Then someone told me that God loved me and would forgive me of all of the wrong things I had done. His Son, Jesus, had paid the penalty for my sins, and all I had to do was ask God to forgive me, and turn from doing wrong to doing what God wanted me to do. That day, I realized a miracle took place when I traded my sin to God for the forgiveness Jesus offered.

My forgiveness as a result of following God's way was the miracle. There is also a miracle yet to come, because I will spend forever with God in heaven. John 3:16 says, "For God so loved the world that he gave his one and only Son, that whoever believes in him shall not perish but have eternal life." Do you know that you do things that disappoint God? You, too, can accept this miracle today. I would love to talk to you later about how you can receive this miracle. Now, let's give away a couple of door prizes, refresh your drinks and popcorn, and get back to the movie.

Refreshments

- Sodas
- Popcorn
- Theatre-style candy

Taking It Home

Candy canes with a note attached that says, "I believe in miracles."

Christmas Around the World

(WorldCrafts Party for Christmas)

Theme

Missions awareness. To host this party, you will need a WorldCrafts Party Kit. To order, call 1-800-968-7301.

WorldCrafts, a nonprofit ministry of WMU, imports handcrafts from countries around the world and markets them in the U.S. When you purchase WorldCrafts items for family and friends, you help provide missionaries with opportunities to share Christ, and you help impoverished craftspeople to provide for their families. The WorldCrafts Party Kit includes catalogs, order forms, a video, recipes, maps, party games, reproducible invitations, and many other helpful resources.

   A WorldCrafts party can be held at any time of the year. The home party below is customized to be a pre-Christmas

WorldCrafts party, a great seasonal party to help you introduce missions and be a witness to your friends and neighbors!

A Party For
Children, youth, or adults

Invitations
(The WorldCrafts Party Kit includes reproducible invitations, or you can make your own using the idea provided below.)

> *'Tis the season to be thinking*
> *Of what you'll give for Christmas.*
> *We will go around the world*
> *To find gifts that are pleasing.*
> *Celebrate Christmas Around the World*
> *With WorldCrafts!*

> *Date:* _____
> *Time:* _____
> *Place:* _____
> *RSVP:* _____

Decorations
Christmas decorations, WorldCrafts maps (included in the party kit), WorldCrafts merchandise that your guests can examine.

Just for Fun
(Game ideas are included in the party kit; you could also use the activity below.)

Bloomers—This is a fun way to keep your guests listening when you do the devotion. Have a small bundle of flowers or a corsage in a peek-proof bag. As your guests listen to your presentation and the video, tell them they are to pass this bagged gift of "bloomers." At the end of the presentation, the guest who is holding the gift will model them. Your guests may be visualizing a giant pair of underwear. They can't imagine having to model them, so they are eager to pass the gift along. Each time the word *WorldCrafts* is spoken, they are to pass the gift to the next guest. At the end of the presentation, the guest holding the bloomers is very relieved when she opens the gift and finds the flowers to model instead.

Devotion

The WorldCrafts Party Kit provides information to introduce your guests to the ministry of WorldCrafts, including a video you can show along with your presentation. You may also use the devotion below.

I am so glad you have come to be a part of our WorldCrafts party. Let me start by saying you are not obligated to purchase anything this evening. I am just glad you came! However, if you see something you like or that meets one of your gift-giving needs, I would love to help you know how you can purchase it.

We are celebrating Christmas Around the World tonight, and Christmas will be here before we know it. The WorldCrafts catalog we will be looking at is full of gift-giving possibilities. The items in WorldCrafts are beautiful and have a satisfaction guarantee—all items are returnable. WorldCrafts is a nonprofit ministry supported and sponsored by WMU. Missionaries all over the world are able to share the love of Christ because of these crafts ministries. WorldCrafts is a different kind of "home party" because, unlike other types of parties, your purchases do not benefit the hostess or a salesperson. Instead, sales of WorldCrafts provide income directly to the artisans who created the merchandise. WorldCrafts enables you to turn your gift buying into missions support! You'll notice in the catalog that the crafts are organized by the nation in which they are produced and the people group to which the artisans belong. A short introduction to each people group is given. The gifts you buy tonight will help missionaries change lives for eternity. (To tell more of the WorldCrafts story, show the video provided in the WorldCrafts Party Kit.)

Thank you again for coming. If you would like to order anything, I have order forms available that you can complete and give to me to send in, or you can take a catalog home with you to decide later. Let me encourage you also to pray for the ministry of WorldCrafts. (Consider distributing copies of the reproducible Prayer Guide included in the WorldCrafts Party Kit.) Or commit to pray for one of these people groups during this Christmas season. I want to give each one of you an ornament or stocking to hang on your tree to help you to remember to pray. On behalf of the artisans and missionaries related to WorldCrafts, thank you for making a difference in their lives. Thanks again for coming.

Refreshments

Refreshments can be made from the recipe cards provided in the WorldCrafts kit. Chex mix, roasted nuts, holiday cookies, and punch could also be used to set a Christmas atmosphere.

Taking It Home

A small ornament or stocking with a note attached that says, "When you see this ornament, I hope you will be reminded to pray for the people group and missionaries you chose at the WorldCrafts party."

Recipes

Recipes

Baked Brims
(Servings according to cake mix directions)

1 box cake mix
icing

Prepare cake batter according to package directions. Grease muffin tins. Fill the tins with enough batter that when they cook the cupcakes will rise and slightly overflow the top of the cups. Bake according to package directions until a toothpick comes out clean. Allow cupcakes to cool on wire rack. Once cooled, slice the top off each cupcake, forming brims for the hats. Ice each brim and place the remaining bottom of each cupcake cut side down on top of the brim. Ice the cupcake to look like a hat. If desired, use colored icing, small candies, or sprinkles to decorate your hats.

Caramel Dip
(Makes 16 servings)

1 16-ounce bag caramels
2 tablespoons evaporated milk
1 8-ounce package cream cheese
Granny Smith apples, sliced

Unwrap all caramel candies and place in a microwave-safe dish. Add evaporated milk and microwave on high for one minute. Stir and add cream cheese. Return to microwave for 30 seconds. Stir. Serve with sliced Granny Smith apples.

Chili Stack Ups
(Makes 16 servings)

1 16-ounce bag tortilla chips
2 16-ounce cans chili con carne with beans
¼ head lettuce, shredded
1 tomato, diced
1 16-ounce bag shredded cheddar cheese
1 10-ounce jar salsa
1 4-ounce jar hot chilies
1 6-ounce jar black olives, sliced
1 8-ounce container sour cream
guacamole

Heat chili, then put everything else out for your guests to stack up on a bed of chips for a delightful treat.

Roll-Ups
(Makes 25 servings)

6 flour tortillas
8 ounces cream cheese
1 tablespoon mayonnaise
¾ cup shredded mild cheddar cheese
¼ cup black olives, chopped
¼ cup jalapeno pepper, chopped
¼ cup green onion, chopped
1 package deli ham

Combine cream cheese, mayonnaise, cheddar cheese, olives, jalapenos, and green onion. Spread mixture over flour tortillas, then lay ham slices on top. Roll tortillas up, then place in a container, seam side down, and refrigerate at least one hour. Slice the rolls thin or thick for appetizers.

Dirt Dessert
(Makes 15 servings)

1 package chocolate sandwich cookies, crushed
1 package (3–4 ounces) chocolate instant pudding
  mix
1 small container (8 ounces) Cool Whip, thawed
1 chocolate and toffee bar (such as Heath), crushed

Make a layer of crushed cookies on the bottom of the
bowl. Prepare pudding according to package directions.
Mix pudding with Cool Whip. Layer the chocolate pudding mixture with the crushed toffee bar. Top off with
another layer of crushed cookies. For fun, you may want
to arrange a few gummy worms on top.

This recipe can be made lighter by using reduced-fat cookies,
fat free pudding mix, and light Cool Whip.

Fiesta Tamale Dip
(Makes 20 servings)

1 15-ounce can tamales, mashed
1 large can chili
2 cups grated mild cheddar cheese
1 16-ounce can refried beans
green chile peppers
round tortilla chips

In a lightly greased dish, layer tamales, chili, cheese,
beans, and green chiles. Bake at 350 degrees until it
bubbles. Serve with tortilla chips.

Friendship Bread and Starter

Starter:

Fill a 3–6 cup jar with **hot water** and let stand. In a saucepan, heat **1 cup 2% milk** in a saucepan to lukewarm (90–100 degrees). Remove from heat and add **3 tablespoons plain, unflavored yogurt**. Drain hot water from jar, dry, and pour in milk/yogurt mixture. Cover tightly. Stand in a warm place. After 18–24 hours, starter should look like yogurt (curd formed). Add **1 cup all-purpose flour** and stir until smooth. Cover and let stand 2–5 days. Starter will smell sour and have small bubbles. Your starter is now ready.

When working with Friendship Starter, use plain, all-purpose flour, a wooden spoon, and do not refrigerate. Start Day 1 of your Friendship Bread.

- *Day 1:* Receive starter and stir with wooden spoon
- *Day 2:* Stir with wooden spoon
- *Day 3:* Stir with wooden spoon
- *Day 4:* Stir with wooden spoon
- *Day 5:* Add 1 cup each of flour, sugar, and milk
- *Day 6:* Stir with wooden spoon
- *Day 7:* Stir with wooden spoon
- *Day 8:* Stir with wooden spoon
- *Day 9:* Stir with wooden spoon
- *Day 10:* Add 1 cup each of flour, sugar, and milk
- *Day 11:* Put 1 cup of starter into each of 3 jars. Give one jar to a friend with instructions on what to do on days 1 through 10. Also include the following instructions for baking the bread. Keep one jar of starter to feed, and use the remaining jar of starter to make bread.

Bread:

To the remaining 1 cup of starter, add the following ingredients.

¾ **cup oil**
2 cups all-purpose flour
1 large package (6 ounces) instant vanilla pudding mix
1 cup sugar
3 eggs
1 teaspoon vanilla extract
1¼ teaspoons baking powder
1 teaspoon baking soda
1 teaspoon salt
1 teaspoon cinnamon
1 cup chopped nuts

Mix together and pour into greased and sugared loaf pans. Bake at 350 degrees for 60 minutes or until done. Cool 10 minutes in pans and remove.

Holiday Cheese Ball
(Makes 20 servings)

2 8-ounce packages cream cheese
1 8½-ounce can crushed pineapple, well drained
2 cups pecans, finely chopped
¼ cup chopped green bell pepper
2 tablespoons chopped onion
1 teaspoon seasoned salt

Soften cream cheese. Gradually stir in drained pineapple, 1 cup chopped pecans, green pepper, onion, and seasoned salt. Chill, then roll ball in the remaining pecans. This will make one large or two small cheese balls.

Fisherman's Folly
(Makes 16 servings)

3¼ cups goldfish crackers
3¼ cups oyster crackers
3¼ cups Cheerios
1⅔ cups peanuts
1⅔ cups pretzel sticks
3 tablespoons margarine
dash garlic powder
ranch salad dressing mix

Combine goldfish crackers, oyster crackers, Cheerios, peanuts, and pretzel sticks. In a small bowl, combine margarine and garlic powder. Microwave on high 20 seconds. Pour over cracker mixture. Sprinkle ranch dressing mix over mixture. Microwave mixture on high for 6 minutes, stirring every 2 minutes.

Friendship Tea
(Makes 20 servings)

2 cups Tang drink mix
1 cup instant tea powder
1 packet presweetened lemonade mix (Kool-Aid)
2½ cups sugar
1 teaspoon ground cloves
1 teaspoon cinnamon

Mix all ingredients together. Store in airtight containers. To serve, stir two heaping teaspoons of dry Friendship Tea mix into a cup of boiling or very hot water. This is a wonderful gift to share with friends.

Hook, Line, and Sinker Dip
(Makes 16 servings)

1 8-ounce package cream cheese
1 8-ounce container sour cream
1 small can shrimp, drained
1 small can crab meat, drained
3 tablespoons seafood cocktail sauce
1 16-ounce bag Fritos Scoops

Mix together the first five ingredients. Serve with "Scoops" chips.

Party Punch
(Makes 30 servings)

6 packages raspberry Kool-Aid (substitute any flavor you want)
6 cups water
6 cups sugar
4 cups sweet tea
2 gallons water
1 large can pineapple juice
1 large can orange juice

Cook the first 3 ingredients over medium heat for 5 minutes, or until sugar dissolves. Mix tea, pineapple juice, and orange juice with the Kool-Aid mixture. Add water, then pour the mixture into gallon-size milk jugs and freeze. Take punch out of freezer about 3 or 4 hours before needed. Cut the tops off the milk jugs to break up the frozen chunks and serve. Yields about 4 gallons. Punch should be served slushy.

Jambalaya
(Makes 10 servings)

2 tablespoons margarine
1½ cups celery, chopped
2 small onions, chopped
½ green bell pepper, diced
1 pound Cajun link sausage, chopped
leftover meat, chopped
1 cup Uncle Ben's converted rice
2 cups water
1½ tablespoons Kitchen Bouquet seasoning sauce
salt, pepper, garlic, red pepper, and soy sauce to taste

Sauté celery, onion, and bell pepper in margarine until tender in a large heavy skillet (a seasoned cast-iron skillet is recommended). In a separate pan, cook chopped sausage and leftover meat portions. Drain excess grease and add the meat to the vegetable mixture in the seasoned skillet. Add rice and two cups water to the meat and vegetables. Season with Kitchen Bouquet, salt, pepper, garlic, red pepper, and soy sauce to your taste. Cook at medium heat for five minutes or until boiling, uncovered. Stir mixture, then cover skillet and simmer on low heat for about 20 minutes. Do not stir or uncover until dish has completed cooking.

Melon Basket

(Makes 16 servings)

1 watermelon
1 cantaloupe melon
1 honeydew melon
1 pint strawberries, washed and quartered
1 pint blueberries, washed

Cut watermelon into the shape of a basket. Dip out melon flesh with melon baller. Cut cantaloupe and honeydew in half and scoop out seeds. Dip out balls or cut into bite-sized chunks. Combine all fruit in the watermelon to serve.

Patriotic Trifle

(Makes 16 servings)

1 angel food cake
1 large package (6 ounces) instant vanilla pudding
  mix
1 large tub (12 ounces) Cool Whip
1 pint fresh strawberries, washed and halved
1 pint fresh blueberries, washed

Prepare vanilla pudding as directed on package. Combine pudding with Cool Whip. Set aside. Tear angel food cake into bite-size pieces. Layer cake, strawberries, pudding mixture, and blueberries. Garnish with berries.

Petite Sandwiches
(Makes 12 servings)

1 loaf white or wheat bread, trimmed of crusts
1 16-ounce package cream cheese,
  or 2 8-ounce packages
1 8-ounce can crushed pineapple, drained

Trim crusts from the bread and cut in halves diagonally, to create triangles. Mix together cream cheese and drained pineapple. Spread on bread and top with a second slice of bread.

You may also make cucumber sandwiches by spreading cream cheese on bread and topping with a slice of cucumber. These cucumber sandwiches are served open-face.

Pumpkin Dip
(Makes 16 servings)

1 8-ounce package cream cheese
½ of 16-ounce can pumpkin (1 cup)
½ teaspoon ground cloves
1 teaspoon cinnamon
¼ cup sugar
1 box ginger snap cookies

Cream together pumpkin, cream cheese, cloves, cinnamon, and sugar. Serve with ginger snaps.

Pumpkin Bread
(Makes 16 servings)

3 cups sugar
3⅓ cups self-rising flour
1 teaspoon cinnamon
½ teaspoon nutmeg
1 16-ounce can pumpkin
1 cup oil
4 eggs
⅔ cup water
1 teaspoon pumpkin pie spice
1 cup pecans, chopped

Combine sugar, self-rising flour, cinnamon, and nutmeg in a bowl. In a separate bowl, mix together pumpkin, oil, eggs, water, and pumpkin pie spice. Combine dry ingredients with pumpkin mixture. Fold in pecans. Preheat oven to 350 degrees. Grease 4 coffee cans or 1 bundt pan. You may also use eight greased soup cans. Fill greased cans ¾ full. Baking time will vary, depending on pans used. Bake until browned and a toothpick inserted in the center comes out clean.

Cheese Grits
(Makes 10 servings)

1 cup quick-cooking grits
½ cup margarine
6 ounces cheese (such as shredded cheddar)
2 eggs, lightly beaten
1 cup milk

Cook grits according to package directions. Add margarine, cheese, eggs, and milk to cooked grits. Pour in a greased pan and bake at 350 degrees for 20 minutes.

Resurrection Cookies
(Makes 3 dozen cookies)

3 egg whites
1 teaspoon white vinegar
⅛ teaspoon cream of tartar
pinch salt
1 cup sugar
1 cup pecans, broken
dash cinnamon

Preheat oven to 350 degrees. Combine egg whites, vinegar, cream of tartar, salt, and sugar. Beat with electric mixer 12–15 minutes until stiff peaks form. Fold in pecans and cinnamon. Drop by teaspoonful onto cookie sheets. Put the cookies in the preheated oven. Turn the oven off and close the door. Seal the door as the stone sealed Jesus' tomb. Let stay in the oven over night. In the morning, remove cookies. You will find they are empty, just as the tomb was empty on Easter morning.

Sweet Treat
(Makes 25 servings)

2 cups Crispix cereal
2 cups Captain Crunch cereal
2 cups pretzel sticks
2 cups roasted, salted peanuts
1 12-ounce package white chocolate chips, melted

Mix dry ingredients in a large bowl. Melt white chocolate chips in microwave for 1 minute. Stir, and return to microwave if not completely melted and smooth. Pour over dry ingredients and stir. Store in an airtight container.

Royal Scones
(Makes 12 servings)

2 cups self-rising flour
¼ cup sugar
⅓ cup margarine
½ cup evaporated milk
1 large egg
1½ teaspoon vanilla extract
1 egg white
1 teaspoon water

Mix flour, sugar, and margarine until crumbled. Combine evaporated milk, egg, and vanilla and beat until mixed. Pour over dry ingredients and stir until moistened. Turn out onto a lightly floured surface and roll out to ½ inch thickness. Using a small round cutter, cut and place on a baking sheet. Whisk together egg white and water to make egg wash. Brush egg wash over tops of scones and sprinkle with colored sugar. Bake at 425 degrees for 13–15 minutes, or until lightly browned.

Colored sugar can be made by putting ¼ cup sugar in a zip-top bag; add several drops food coloring and work coloring into sugar.

Mini Biscuits

Prepare Bisquick mix or other biscuit mix according to package directions. Bake biscuits (according to directions) in a mini muffin pan to make bite-sized biscuits.

Tea Time Cookies
(Makes 24 servings)

1½ sticks butter or margarine, softened
⅔ cup sugar
1 egg
1 teaspoon vanilla extract
¼ teaspoon salt
1¾ cups all-purpose flour, sifted
½ cup pecans, finely chopped

Cream together butter and sugar. Beat in egg, vanilla, and salt. Gradually stir in flour. Shape dough into 2 rolls about 1½ inches in diameter and 6 inches long. Roll each in ¼ cup chopped pecans to coat outside. Wrap in plastic wrap; chill thoroughly. Cut into slices ¼ inch thick. Place on ungreased cookie sheets. Bake in preheated 350 degree oven for 15 to 17 minutes or until lightly browned.